WHO NEEDS A MISSIONARY?

Who Needs a Missionary?

How the Gospel Can Work All by Itself

Robert Reese

RESOURCE *Publications* · Eugene, Oregon

WHO NEEDS A MISSIONARY?
How the Gospel Can Work All by Itself

Copyright © 2014 Robert Reese. All rights reserved. Except for brief quotations in critical publications or reviews, no part of this book may be reproduced in any manner without prior written permission from the publisher. Write: Permissions, Wipf and Stock Publishers, 199 W. 8th Ave., Suite 3, Eugene, OR 97401.

Resource Publications
An Imprint of Wipf and Stock Publishers
199 W. 8th Ave., Suite 3
Eugene, OR 97401

www.wipfandstock.com

ISBN 13: 978-1-62564-358-2

Manufactured in the U.S.A.

All scripture quotations are taken from the Holy Bible, New International Version®, NIV®. Copyright © 1973, 1978, 1984 by Biblica, Inc.™ Used by permission of Zondervan. All rights reserved worldwide.

Contents

Foreword vii

Preface ix

Prologue 1

1 Conversion 5

2 Training 22

3 Church Planting 46

4 Making a Living 71

5 Obstacles and Suffering 87

6 Training Leaders 106

7 Transforming the Community 121

8 Rebuilding the Walls 145

Epilogue 159

Bibliography 163

Foreword

In his book, *Who Needs a Missionary?*, Robert Reese takes us on an extraordinary journey as he describes the spiritual and personal maturing of a remarkable Zimbabwean Christian leader named Isaac Ndendela. If his personal story was written as Christian fiction, most people might be tempted to say, "Great story, but it simply couldn't happen in real life." But it did happen, and it is continuing to happen.

Isaac Ndendela was born and grew up in a very remote village in the northwestern part of rural Zimbabwe. "Remote" and "rural" do not adequately convey the context of a culture rooted in animism, ancestor worship, and witchcraft. While the people were very hard-working, warm, and hospitable, Christianity had not yet come to his village.

As a young boy he was forced to drop out of school after less than one year of education in order to take care of the family goats and to help farm the land designated for his family. Eventually, he sought work in Bulawayo, some three hundred miles away from home. At that point his life began to take some twists and turns that could only be described as directed by God. He was not a Christian when he arrived, but God clearly had a plan for him.

The journey from Isaac becoming a "babe in Christ" to eagerly wanting to return home to take the gospel of Christ to his family and his entire village will thrill you as you read it. Robert Reese outlines how God continued to transform Isaac from his humble beginnings to an outstanding Christian leader, evangelist, church planter, mentor, devoted husband, loving father, and highly respected community leader.

While the book primarily is devoted to the fascinating personal journey of Isaac Ndendela, it is also an excellent tutorial on the very practical challenges and joys of cross-cultural mission work in general. I can assure you that everyone involved in one way or another in mission programs will be energized and encouraged by the story of Isaac Ndendela. It has been my great pleasure to accompany Robert Reese on six short-term mission trips

Foreword

to Zimbabwe. During each trip it always is a great joy to visit with Isaac and see the wonderful respect he has gained among his peers as he continues to carry the gospel of Christ to his people.

George Bragg
Irvine, California

Preface

Almost from the beginning of our mission work in Zimbabwe, we got to know Isaac Ndendela. My wife and I arrived as missionaries in Bulawayo in 1981 and returned to the USA in 2002. Within our first year in Zimbabwe we had met Isaac, but the idea of writing his story only began to take shape near the end of our time there. Over two decades had passed where we were able to observe his character and actions, from the time just after his conversion to a time when he had helped plant five churches. While there are many stories we could tell about a multitude of other Christ-followers, something stands out about Isaac.

The first few years after we arrived back in the USA, I would travel in the summers out to our original sponsoring church, Creekside Christian Fellowship (now called Journey Christian Church), in California to prepare a small team that would travel with me to Zimbabwe for a short-term mission. Those annual trips to Creekside Christian Fellowship gave me opportunities to speak on Sunday morning to the whole church. On one such occasion, I told Isaac's story and related it to the Parable of the Growing Seed in Mark 4:26–29. In that parable, the farmer plants the seed and then has very little to do with its growth, as it grows all by itself. That seemed to describe Isaac's ministry, since he came to follow Christ without a missionary and with only the simplest form of gospel seed imaginable.

When I presented this story, the Creekside members gave such affirming feedback that I asked some of them what the difference was between that sermon and others I had given before. The answer I got was that this time I told a story from real life and tied it to Scripture. From then on, I decided to research Isaac's life more deeply, looking for the spiritual lessons from which others could benefit.

Of course, that was easier said than done, since Isaac has lived in a rather remote part of Zimbabwe since 1987, while I now live in the USA. Nonetheless, some teams from Creekside Christian Fellowship went with

Preface

me to Isaac's village a couple of times and I continued to meet Isaac once a year at the annual Bible schools we conducted in Bulawayo. Then in 2010, I hired an eighteen-year-old driver with a pickup truck to take me to Isaac's home. We slept in small tents near a shed built to keep the midday sun off, eating what the Tonga people ate. During the day, my teenage driver would wander off into the nearby hills with local Tonga boys, while I participated in a Bible school that met under the shed. Each evening I sat down with Isaac for a long conversation about his life in Christ. From those extensive interviews came the heart of this book.

Much of what you are about to read contains Isaac's personal recollections about his conversion and ministry. Sometimes I supplemented his memories, which were not only clear but also detailed, with items from my personal diary or our missionary newsletters to establish timelines and events. But I did not consult anyone else, since I really wanted to let Isaac speak for himself. For a long time I have felt that the voices of people like Isaac need to be heard, since they rarely have a public voice beyond their own isolated ministries. This gave an opportunity to see what the highlights were from his point of view of his life in Christ, how he thought of ministry, and what kept him going.

Of course, I also have my own agenda, so I organized Isaac's comments into chapters that also contain supporting episodes from other people's lives. And since I am a teacher, I could not resist making Isaac's experiences into lessons for others. After the narrative in each chapter, I make some personal observations, using Scripture to establish some spiritual lessons about that aspect of Isaac's life. Perhaps the most important lesson I drew from his life is that the gospel does have a power of its own that literally works by itself even in the absence of a missionary.

The ideas for this book have been on my mind for a long time. The fact that they are just now being published is because of the help of a number of people. First and foremost are my daughter, Charlotte, and her husband Sam Myung, who edited the entire manuscript. Then there are the editors and publishers at Wipf and Stock in Oregon. And finally, Isaac Ndendela provided the details that make this story what it is. For the whole experience of getting this book into print, I am deeply grateful to all these people; to God be the glory!

Prologue

The history of Christian missions is replete with famous names, such as William Carey, Adoniram and Ann Judson, David Livingstone, Hudson and Maria Taylor, Amy Carmichael, and many more. Most of these well-known missionaries were from the West and went out to exotic lands in Africa and Asia sometime in the past two hundred years. Much is known about their lives because they were often prolific writers who documented their efforts for the cause of Christ. Textbooks on mission history would never leave out such valuable material, but do these heroes tell the whole story?

Having taught the history of missions for the past decade, I often ask students to tell me the names of famous missionaries they have heard about. The usual names always come up, and I encourage students to select a biography of their favorite missionary and write a book report on it as one of their graded assignments. But one day, when I asked students that question, a young man raised his hand and said his favorite missionary was Dr. Brown. When I replied that I was unaware who Dr. Brown was, he explained, "He was my grandfather." That brings up an important point about the history of missions: the vast majority of missionaries throughout the past twenty centuries are unknown to most people.

Even in the New Testament, unknown missionaries were prominent in spreading the gospel after the death and resurrection of Christ. While the cross-cultural ministry of the apostle Paul is emphasized in the Book of Acts, others are also mentioned but not named. The first multicultural church in the world was located in Antioch, where followers of Christ were first called Christians (Acts 11:26), probably because they were no longer easily categorized as a sect of Judaism. So who founded the church in Antioch? Acts 11:20 says, "Some of them [those scattered by the persecution that followed the martyrdom of Stephen], however, men from Cyprus and Cyrene, went to Antioch and began to speak to Greeks also, telling them the good news about the Lord Jesus." We will never know the names of those early missionaries until the end of time, but the initial work they did reverberated for centuries as Antioch became a major missionary-sending church to multiple cultures in Europe and Asia.

Similarly, I have often heard that the apostle Paul was the first to bring the gospel to Europe, but that is actually untrue. By the time Paul saw the vision of the man of Macedonia in Acts 16:9, there was already a church in Rome. We see that clearly in Acts 18:2, where Paul is continuing his inaugural missionary journey into Europe and meets Aquila and Priscilla in Corinth. That Christian missionary couple had recently been expelled from Rome! Now they eagerly joined Paul in his mission efforts. So how did the church in Rome get its start? Again it must be unnamed missionaries, although Aquila and Priscilla may have entered the picture at an early stage. From Acts 2:10, we see that Jews from Rome were present in Jerusalem when the Holy Spirit fell on the followers of Christ on the Day of Pentecost. No doubt some of them became Christians that day and very likely would have returned to Rome, spreading the gospel message to fellow Jews there as well as to Gentiles; Paul seems to refer to contentious issues between Jews and Gentiles in Rome in his letter to the churches in that city (Rom 14:1—15:13). Church history emphasizes the importance of the church in Rome, but we do not know who actually planted the first assembly of Christians there.

Apart from these examples taken from the Book of Acts, there are many similar examples from mission history. To take one example, consider the work of Adoniram and Ann Judson in Burma. Although their dedication to God's work was outstanding, and the suffering they had to endure was extreme, the real breakthrough in reaching a segment of the people of Burma came through an indigenous convert named Ko Tha Byu.[1] While the Judsons' ministry is well-known, the ministry of Ko Tha Byu is not. The latter was from the Karen tribe of Burma; Judson found him as a debt-slave in 1827, ransomed and freed him from slavery. Samuel Moffett describes him as "not only a thief but a murderer who admitted to killing at least thirty men."[2] Once Ko Tha Byu became a Christian, he wasted no time in evangelizing his own Karen people. By the time of his death in 1840,

---

1. Moffett, *History of Christianity in Asia*, 322–28.
2. Ibid., 327.

he had been responsible for 1,270 conversions, the beginning of a famous people movement to Christ among the Karens.[3]

This book is the story of Isaac Ndendela, a Zimbabwean convert to Christ, who is unknown except by those relative few his ministry has touched. The results of his life are not as spectacular as those of Ko Tha Byu, but they are still significant in his part of the world. He will never be cited in a book on the history of missions because his sphere of influence is too small. But he serves to show how the gospel works in people of various cultures when they understand and respond positively to it.

African scholar, Lamin Sanneh, who is also a professor at Yale University, cites two distinct aspects of the spread of Christianity through missions. The first is what mission historians write in their books, which Sanneh calls the "historic transmission" of the gospel. This aspect deals with the key missionaries who took the gospel to remote or unreached places, and it has been chronicled thoroughly. The other aspect Sanneh calls "indigenous assimilation," which is the response by indigenous peoples to the message as they understood it.[4] This part of the transmission of Christianity has not been reported as extensively, but it is in fact the more important aspect, since it entails the indigenous acceptance and use of the message of the gospel.

One reason that hardly anyone knows about Isaac's work for the Lord is that he cannot express himself well in English, having withdrawn from school during the first grade to herd the family's goats. He is self-educated and taught himself to read not only his own language, Tonga, but also a few others. With respect to education and privilege, Isaac has neither, and so it is not surprising he is unknown. What is surprising is how the gospel affected him and how he responded to it. No missionary taught him the gospel, but rather the seed of the gospel entered his heart in a remarkable way and worked all by itself. That is the subject matter of this book.

Searching for a biblical way to grasp what happened in Isaac's life, I found a short parable of Jesus that helped me to understand. Mark 4:26–29 is unique to Mark's gospel and it applies directly to Isaac's conversion experience:

> He [Jesus] also said, "This is what the kingdom of God is like. A man scatters seed on the ground. Night and day, whether he sleeps or gets up, the seed sprouts and grows, though he does not know

3. Ibid., 328.
4. Sanneh, "Horizontal and Vertical in Mission," 166.

how. All by itself the soil produces grain—first the stalk, then the head, then the full kernel in the head. As soon as the grain is ripe, he puts the sickle to it, because the harvest is come."

The kingdom of God is defined as God's rule. In what we know as the Lord's Prayer, there are parallel lines that say, "Your kingdom come, your will be done on earth as it is in heaven" (Matt 6:10). This defines God's kingdom as being where God's will is done, in other words, where God rules. In another place, Jesus said, "But if I drive out demons by the Spirit of God, then the kingdom of God has come upon you" (Matt 12:28). In this context of spiritual warfare, when Jesus was driving out demons, clearly he was attacking Satan's kingdom where God's will was being disregarded in order to bring in God's kingdom.

The Parable of the Growing Seed in Mark 4:26–29 says that God's kingdom is like a man scattering seed on the ground. In Isaac's case, he was far from obedience to God and outside God's kingdom when he found a gospel tract, literally scattered on the ground in order to shatter Satan's grip and establish God's rule in his life. From that point on, Isaac could not rest until he had figured out how to respond to what he read. Notice again that the seed has a power of its own, so that whether the farmer is awake or asleep, the seed grows. The farmer may control some aspects of cultivation, such as weeding, watering, aerating, and fertilizing, but he or she can never control the seed. God moves in sovereign and mysterious ways to bring his kingdom into people's lives; he runs the mission.

That is why the subtitle of this book is "How the Gospel Can Work All by Itself." The Parable of the Growing Seed in Mark 4:26–29 is really about the work of God in someone's life to bring not only the kingdom or rule of God into that life but also to spread it to others; that is Isaac's story. The wonder of Isaac's life is how God can use anyone who opens himself or herself up to God, being available and willing to serve him, no matter what the cost. That is what will bring in the final harvest when the multiplication of seeds results in overwhelming bounty, as mentioned in the last verse of this powerful parable. Apart from such Scriptures it is difficult to understand the dramatic changes that the gospel brought to Isaac's life.

1

Conversion

We first met Isaac Ndendela near the village of Esigodini in Zimbabwe. "Village" is used in the English sense of a small town, not in the African sense of a cluster of huts. Esigodini has a rustic Anglican chapel that could have been plucked from an English village. Right next to it is a cricket pitch with the white backboards that are there to enhance the batter's ability to see the dark red ball coming. Originally, Esigodini was named Essexvale, and was set up as a small business center for white farmers in a broad valley with several dams that supply nearby Bulawayo with water and also allow for some irrigated farming.

By 1981, when we arrived in Zimbabwe, life in Esigodini was beginning to change. As a nation, Zimbabwe had only been created one year earlier after a long guerrilla war. The newly elected government headed by Robert Mugabe began by changing the names of towns in a symbolic gesture to move away from the colonial past. Essexvale became Esigodini, a word meaning "in the valley" in the local Ndebele language. Beyond that, shops began to cater more to the African population, since they were in the clear majority and now seemed to be in charge of the country. Slowly but surely, Esigodini was being transformed into an African town.

My wife, Mari-Etta, and I rented a house in Esigodini from the Electricity Supply Commission (ESC) right on the main highway from Bulawayo to Johannesburg. As 1981 was a year of transition in Zimbabwe, white people were leaving in droves from fear of an imminent Communist revolution, since Mugabe was and is a self-proclaimed Marxist. This created a brain drain from parastatals like the ESC and opened the way for a missionary couple to have one of their houses for a year.

Who Needs a Missionary?

Our goal was to study the language and culture of the Ndebele people before diving into fulltime church planting. Ironically, an Ndebele woman we had met in the United States had recommended Esigodini as an ideal place to learn the language and she was right. Many Ndebele lived in Esigodini, where they worked for white people or shopkeepers, and just over the range of hills to the south were the communal lands where traditional Ndebele villages abounded.

Our colleagues in mission, Allen and Janelle Avery, had arrived before us and established an English-speaking church in their house. In 1981, this congregation was predominantly composed of white people who were making an effort to adjust to the changes in the country. In fact, the dramatic turn of events leading to independence for the country caused many white people to open up to the gospel for the first time. Losing the sense of privilege caused many to think about God and their own spiritual condition.

One of those who turned to Christ in a deep and abiding way was Sandy Wolhuter. She and her husband Geoff ran a chicken farm near Esigodini. They had one child at that time, as we did. Their Jeremy and our Ellen were almost identical in age, under a year old when we first met. As both our families continued to have children, they always seemed to match in age. Since Sandy worshipped with us on Sundays and our children brought us together, we began to visit the Wolhuters regularly as they lived close by.

Going to the Wolhuters' place from our house in the valley, we would drive towards Bulawayo on the main highway, reaching a steep ascent known locally as "Danger." Zimbabwe always seemed to have vehicles on the road that belonged in a museum, so the biggest danger seemed to be that the drive up the hills would be the death of the vehicle. My main memory of "Danger" is seeing vehicle engines boiling over on the uphill stretch. No doubt there was also the danger of speeding (or "overspeeding," as the Zimbabweans phrased it) on the winding downhill drive.

Just beyond the summit, we would turn to go down again into a steep valley where the Wolhuters had their farm. Their Dutch-styled farmhouse, which never seemed quite finished, nestled in the bottom of what the locals called "*esihotsheni,*" meaning "in the gulch." In winter, the chill from the surrounding hills would funnel down like a cold blanket where the afternoon sun couldn't reach. That is where we met Isaac, who worked as foreman for the chicken farm.

Conversion

Isaac is a Tonga man from the hot and steamy Zambezi River valley in northern Zimbabwe along the border with Zambia. In fact, the Tonga people live on both sides of that great river that forms the border, since the national boundaries were drawn by Europeans who had little or no idea about the groups of people they were dividing up into new "nations."

Most of the year, the Tongas need no blankets, because as the Africans say, "The heat is the poor person's blanket." Indeed, the Tongas tend to be poor and somewhat despised by other groups in Zimbabwe. Their region was only opened up with roads during the building of the Kariba Dam on the Zambezi River in the late 1950s. Even into the twenty-first century some Tongas still live in much the same way as their ancestors. Compared to urbanized Africans, Tongas are often thought of as country bumpkins.

Having been born in Zimbabwe of American missionary parents, I occasionally traveled through Tonga territory as a boy and I remember stopping now and then at a fly gate. This was an attempt to halt the spread of the tsetse fly, the carrier of sleeping sickness. The fly's sting is like that of a horse fly, but more painful, a fact I know from personal experience. Mainly, however, the sting means death for most domesticated animals. This meant that the Tongas had no cattle, which abounded elsewhere in Zimbabwe. At the fly gate, the vehicle drove into an enclosed and darkened shed so that any flies riding on it would move toward the windows and be trapped. At the same time, the attendants would spray insecticide underneath the vehicle to kill any remaining flies.

By the twenty-first century, the fly gates had become a thing of the past, as the tsetse fly was sufficiently eradicated. Tongas were also becoming more engaged with the outside world. The modern world means the market economy. Families now need cash to pay school fees for their children, and to buy things like soap, matches, cooking oil, tea, and sugar. These new necessities drove Tonga men to find jobs far from home. Even though Isaac did not yet have his own family, he joined the migration out of the remote Zambezi River valley and went to the Bulawayo area, the center of Ndebele culture, over three hundred miles south of his home.

Isaac quite enjoyed the bright lights of Zimbabwe's second largest city. At that time, just prior to Zimbabwe gaining independence in 1980, Bulawayo was a city of about half a million people. Independence meant greater opportunities for Africans, so they were flocking to the urban areas where globalization had begun to concentrate jobs. For people familiar with international urbanization, Bulawayo still seems provincial and laconic, a bit of a colonial throwback in the modern era. But for Isaac it was quite a refreshing change from his earlier days in the bush. He was interested in more than jobs, however, as were many young men first arriving in the big city.

Soon Isaac was living with a new girlfriend in a room he rented in the sprawling western suburbs of Bulawayo. That side of town was part of Zimbabwe's colonial legacy of enforced racial segregation in housing. The western suburbs were quite literally on the wrong side of the tracks, as the railway line from Botswana to Harare, Zimbabwe's capital city, split the city in two. To the east of the railway line were the spacious yards of the eastern suburbs, reserved for white people in colonial times. To the west were the tiny "match-box" houses originally built as cheap rental homes for urban laborers of the lower classes. In the middle were located Bulawayo's factories and heavy industries, dominated by the railways. The prevailing southeast wind tended to blow industrial pollution toward the western areas. Even when the eastern suburbs were thrown open to residents of all races, the western suburbs remained uniformly high density low-cost African housing. To these western areas the vast majority of new urban dwellers came to find cheap housing, causing these areas to expand rapidly in the postcolonial period. Along with the expansion came all the familiar urban vices.

Isaac enjoyed his vices in his new location. He had the common Tonga habit of smoking marijuana, or *imbanje* as it is called in Zimbabwe. *Imbanje* smoking is so entrenched among Tongas that the government decided not to combat it. Thus they made Tonga territory the only part of Zimbabwe where *imbanje* is legalized. Other groups also smoked the weed, but they ran the risk of being arrested for it. Of course, even Tongas were not allowed to export this crop nor to smoke it when away from their home area, but many still did. Isaac was one of them. He was used to indulging in a number of harmful habits.

One day while Isaac was out in the small yard of his home in the suburb of Pelandaba, he spotted a paper lying in the garden. When he picked it up he realized it was a Christian tract in a series entitled "Voice of Prophecy." However, it was written in the Shona language, the tongue of the majority group in Zimbabwe, and he couldn't read it. Intrigued nonetheless, he filled out the response sheet and mailed it in, effectively enrolling himself in a correspondence course that he could not understand.

Isaac was a first-grade dropout in school. After Isaac spent a single term in first grade, his father pulled him out to do something more useful:

herd goats. As a result, Isaac grew up illiterate, although he had learned the alphabet during that brief sojourn in school. When he became an adult, he realized the necessity of teaching himself to read his own Tonga language. Now he was determined to learn to read and speak Shona in order to study the Voice of Prophecy lessons.

The lessons began to arrive with all Shona words and no pictures. The teacher identified himself as J. J. Muganda, saying at the outset that Isaac had chosen to enroll in a good school. He urged that every student should pray at precisely 8:00 am daily in order to join in this exercise with all other students. As a result, daily morning prayer would become an entrenched habit for Isaac, but for now he was only beginning to try to pray. However, the issue that opened his mind up was the third thing that J. J. Muganda emphasized. He asked, "Do you own a Bible? If not, borrow one and read it." Muganda also emphasized the danger of breaking God's laws in the Bible.

The tract that Isaac found was hardly the kind of literature that would normally convince anyone to become a Christian, because it was extremely negative. It was direct and hard-hitting, condemning every sin that Isaac was in the habit of doing, in no uncertain terms. Sexual immorality, drunkenness, drug addictions, theft, lying, cheating, and so on would all consign a person to certain torment in hell on Judgment Day.

Isaac mulled over these words in the first lesson, but carried on with his life as before. One day, as he was spending time with his girlfriend in his tiny room, he glanced down to see the tract lying there. He had been carrying it around with him and now it was on the bed where he was about to have sex with his mistress. He suddenly thought again about what he was doing and the warnings from the tract. "Do you believe in God's laws?" the tract asked. Here he was, about to commit fornication and with some plugs of *imbanje* in his pocket. J. J. Muganda seemed to know all about his sinful life. Suddenly, he took fright and in that moment decided to repent of all his sins and make a fresh start in life.

He understood that Christianity called for a change of behavior. He told his girlfriend that they could no longer engage in sexual relations because he was now a Christian. He didn't chase her away, but told her not to expect him to act towards her as he had been doing. He told her she was welcome to sleep in their bed as before but he would no longer feel free to touch her as he had been doing. He was really determined to make a clean break with the past.

Who Needs a Missionary?

Since he knew very little about Christianity, he decided to invest in a Bible, as Muganda had been urging him. At the Matopo Book Centre, he was so excited about owning his own Tonga Bible that he left the store without even waiting for his change after he paid the cashier. Reading was laborious for him and he only did it because he was now looking for answers to his many questions. The tract had told him to accept Jesus as his Savior and Lord so that he could be forgiven for his sins, and he knew that he desperately needed that. He was a broken man, and he kept his resolve to quit having sex with his girlfriend. She only stayed a week sleeping in his bed without physical relations and then left.

Isaac continued with the Voice of Prophecy correspondence course until he had completed all thirty lessons. He now proudly displays the certificate of completion of the course on his wall. He even managed to see his teacher, J. J. Muganda, at a church service in Bulawayo, but he didn't introduce himself because of his shy manner. Muganda had notified his correspondence students that he would be in Bulawayo on a certain day, and Isaac went to see him out of curiosity. But he still had no church and many questions remained about following Christ. It was during this time of uncertainty that he met Geoff and Sandy Wolhuter.

Isaac's first impression of Geoff was a negative one. Geoff roared up on his motorcycle to check his mailbox at the Leighton Post Office near the main railway station while Isaac happened to be there. Geoff had long hair, a beard, and an abrupt manner. That day he was looking for farm workers and he went straight up to Isaac to ask if he wanted work. Isaac could understand his English but had trouble replying in English. Although he didn't trust this strange white man, he warily agreed to wait for Geoff to return with transport to take him to the farm.

Soon Geoff was back with his wife, Sandy, who was driving their car. Geoff told Isaac to get in the car with Sandy so he could take up his new lodgings on the farm, and off they went. When he arrived at the farm he wasn't sure he would like this isolated place working for this unusual man. The other workers seemed to confirm his worst fears; they told Isaac that Geoff was mad. Nevertheless this crazy white man soon handed Isaac some blankets and food and showed him to his living quarters.

Isaac, like a few hundred thousand other Zimbabweans, found employment on one of the four thousand white-owned farms. Although the government was supposed to be Marxist, real economic power still rested in white hands, just as it had during the colonial era. Zimbabwe was still divided up between white farms and communal lands. This was not just a theoretical division but was actually visible when moving around the country.

As one passed from white farmlands into communal lands, usually marked by a cattle grid (or guard), it was like passing from park to desert. The visible difference between commercial farms and communal areas came from the effects of overgrazing by too many livestock in the African zones. White farms, on the other hand, looked underutilized and pristine by comparison, even though they too had some African villages where farm workers lived. Communal lands were often organized in "lines," meaning lines of villages with fields on one side of the line of huts, and livestock on the other side where there might also be a source of surface water like a dam. The idea was that all Africans who lived there shared communal grazing and waterholes for their livestock. Each family was allocated fields according to their needs by the local chief or headman.

By the time Isaac arrived at the Wolhuters' farm, he had begun to mingle successfully with the other dominant language groups by learning to speak both Shona and Ndebele. He had met and married Margaret Mhlanga, an Ndebele woman from the nearby Sigola communal lands. She gave him his first child, Nomsa, a name meaning "with grace" in Ndebele, indicating how God had smiled on them with the gift of a daughter. She was almost identical in age to both our daughter Ellen and the Wolhuters' son, Jeremy.

The Wolhuters gave him work in the chicken house with the responsibility of raising chicks. At first he handled a hundred newborn chicks a month, but that number increased to a thousand per month. He began to prove himself more trustworthy than the other employees by faithfully reporting to Geoff each chick that died in his care. In this way, he soon worked his way up to being foreman of the farm.

As his mentor, J. J. Muganda, had urged, he began a daily habit of going off into the bush alone each morning to pray before work. One day, as he was praying under an *umdwadwa* tree, he felt that he had been transported several yards without initiating it himself. He simply closed his eyes as he was praying fervently and when he opened them he was no longer where he had started praying. At times he would go from kneeling to standing without realizing it. He couldn't explain the movement, but neither could he understand exactly how prayer or worship worked. He hunched down lower and began to pray loudly to the God of the universe. He was not aware that Sandy Wolhuter had noticed him and was spying on him.

Who Needs a Missionary?

Sandy was having tea with some visiting ladies that morning out in her front yard when the group heard what sounded like wailing coming from the bush. The ladies scanned the bush across the small stream that ran near the house, but couldn't make out where the noise was coming from. Sandy went and got her binoculars to get a better look. She spotted Isaac, who was in fervent prayer, moaning so loudly that it sounded like shouting. She was completely amazed, as she had not even known that he was a believer!

The next day, when Isaac came to the back door of the Wolhuters' house to get the keys he would need to begin working, he found Sandy waiting for him. "Isaac, what were you doing out in the bush yesterday morning? It looked like you were praying." He was taken aback, as he had not realized how far the sounds had carried, or that anyone had seen him. "I was watching you through the binoculars," Sandy continued. "You were praying, weren't you?" "No, madam," he stammered, "I don't know how to pray or worship." Sandy replied, "That's exactly what you were doing."

Isaac proceeded to tell Sandy about his desire to follow Christ. But he added that he was struggling to figure out how to pray and worship, as he had no experience to go by. Sandy replied, "Isaac, you are already praying and worshipping. What you need is to come with me to our worship service next Sunday to see how other Christians worship and pray together."

That is how Isaac came to worship with us and to become a member of our church. He recognized right away that what took place in the church service was what he had instinctively done alone in the bush. Now he had found a group of believers to belong to where he could grow as a disciple of Jesus. A few weeks later, an evangelist named Elliot Donga came out to the farm to baptize Isaac in the stream that ran close to the Wolhuters' house.

Isaac remained eager to learn more, so that he could follow his new Lord more closely. What began without any intermediary or human intervention, except for those unknown people like J. J. Muganda who wrote and distributed the Voice of Prophecy, developed into a fellowship of committed Christians for Isaac.

The Meaning of Conversion

Have you noticed how conversions to Christ are not all the same? When a person like Isaac comes along proving his deep commitment to Christ from the beginning in ways that overshadow the commitment of others, it begs the question, What is the difference? Isaac, a first-grade dropout, shows that education has nothing to do with it, or perhaps that too much education can hinder a deep conversion. Additionally, he proves that being poor and despised has nothing to do with it, or that coming from the low end of the pecking order might even help in conversion. But what I would like to investigate here is a cultural model for how spiritualists come to Christ, because Isaac came from a purely spiritualistic worldview.

Spiritualist is another word for "animist." One editor told me that the term "animist" is offensive to some people. Whenever we try to analyze other cultures, we run the risk of offending the very people we are trying to understand. Thus the need to keep changing our terms of reference in the postcolonial era when multiple viewpoints vie for acceptance.

Spiritualist refers to the dominance of spirits in this worldview. By worldview, we mean the set of assumptions a person has about reality. These assumptions help to determine how people react to various challenges. For example, when my wife and I arrived in Esigodini, I took as language helper a man named Agrippa Moyo, who was definitely a spiritualist and not a Christian. By language helper, I mean he was not my teacher in the formal Western sense. That would have implied a classroom with Agrippa deciding on a curriculum. He was rather my teacher in an African sense of spending time together as I struggled to put what I wanted to say into Ndebele, Agrippa's mother tongue. Agrippa not only helped me phrase my thoughts in his language, but he provided invaluable insight into his culture. The fact that Agrippa was not a Christian helped me to see the perspective of pure spiritualism that I would have missed otherwise. This was never more the case than when his wife became so ill she was admitted to the local mental asylum.

By that time, we had left Esigodini and moved into Bulawayo. Agrippa had completed his work of teaching me Ndebele and was now a good friend. He lived in a communal area called Mawabeni down the road from Esigodini and eked out a living raising crops and livestock. We now lived in Famona, a former all-white suburb of Bulawayo that was becoming a mixed race neighborhood, as its houses were affordable at that time. At the end of our short street was a large field with hospital buildings visible in the distance. This was the famous Engutsheni Hospital, the main psychiatric facility for all of Zimbabwe.

When I was a schoolboy growing up in Harare, the nation's capital three hundred miles north of Bulawayo, we had a repertoire of jokes about

Who Needs a Missionary?

Engutsheni as the rightful dwelling place of all crazy people in Zimbabwe. Now we lived within sight of it, and the large field around it was to deter inmates who often tried to escape. Nevertheless, we would occasionally see them running down our street with hospital orderlies usually in hot pursuit.

Agrippa's wife gave birth to a chubby baby girl named Busi and then went into some sort of mental illness that landed her in Engutsheni. We didn't see her in that initial condition, but only heard that she was now our neighbor in Famona and that she needed help. Agrippa's family brought Busi to live with us so that we could take the baby over to Engutsheni once a day for breastfeeding, to prevent the mother's milk from drying up while she was receiving treatment. But treatment for what?

Now we got an inside look into that renowned hospital, filled with people in a pitiful state of mind, many heavily sedated, and this included Agrippa's wife. She didn't resist nursing, so was able to continue to nurse her baby after she was released. When we asked the nurses what was wrong with her, they replied that she had postpartum depression. But to a traditional African, this Western medical description made little sense. Why should a woman suddenly become sad after giving birth? Did she want to be eternally pregnant?

When we asked Agrippa what had happened to his wife, he had a different explanation: she had walked out of their hut one evening and seen an owl. That of course raises further questions. What did the owl mean? Naturally, nocturnal creatures are somehow mysterious and associated with dark activities. In Africa, such creatures as the owl, hyena, and antbear are regarded as either emanations of evil spirits or transport for witches. In either case, their appearance creates the fear that someone is planning to do evil against the one who sees them.

Agrippa not only claimed that his wife had seen an owl just before she went insane, but he also knew a likely culprit who brought this illness on her. A witch in this cultural context is potentially anyone who bears a grudge, since grudges can develop into witchcraft. Jealousy and envy are the main reasons for witchcraft, as the suspicion that someone else is outdoing you may drive you to evil thoughts of trying to bring that person down. Thoughts of causing harm to someone can bring about witchcraft either intentionally or unintentionally, since the evil can take on a life of its own.

In the case of giving birth, it is easy to see that any barren women could be jealous. Agrippa lived right next to his maternal uncle as his mother's family had raised him. This uncle had two wives, the elder of whom had no children. This is the person Agrippa blamed for his wife's condition. But it was not a public accusation, as that would require an expert, such as an *inyanga*, to sniff out the witch. The *inyanga* was a traditional spiritualist practitioner who could communicate with the spirit world to find answers for questions like what had caused Agrippa's wife to be ill. If Agrippa did not want to pay for this expert's services, he would have to bear his own grudge secretly against his uncle's first wife. In this way, witchcraft secretly feeds on itself and perpetuates divisions.

Can there be any understanding between the modern Western explanation of postpartum depression and the spiritualist explanation of witchcraft? Probably not, because these two worldviews have so little in common. In fact, this is a good illustration of basic differences between a secular western worldview and a spiritualist worldview that many Africans, Asians, and Latin Americans have. Reality for a person brought up with a Western mindset is in the scientific analysis of a problem like sickness, whereas it lies in the spirit world for an African.

What happens when a Western missionary from a secular orientation, like me, tries to bring a spiritualist like Agrippa to faith in Jesus Christ? There are several possible responses, ranging from outright rejection to deep conversion. Notice that outright rejection might actually be misunderstanding. The spiritualist and secularist have no meeting of the minds and so rejection could simply be a lack of comprehension. On the other hand, rejection might come from the perception that the Christian worldview means the collapse of the spiritualist worldview and all it stands for.

One day when I was doing evangelism door-to-door with two young African trainees in the Emakhandeni suburb of Bulawayo, we arrived at a dwelling where the lady of the house was home with her children. She was receptive to the gospel and we were making real progress until her husband arrived home. He saw the open Bibles, the white missionary, and African lads and walked past us into his bedroom. When he returned, he did not look pleased. The thing I did not notice—and one of the reasons I found it helpful to work closely with African brothers—is that the man of the house came out with his right hand in a tight fist. What I did notice was that he was decidedly hostile to us. As he gripped what turned out to be snuff in his right hand, he told us that he and his family had no need of the white man's Jesus, whom he understood to be an ancestral spirit of Europeans. We politely dismissed ourselves and left. My African helpers explained that the snuff was typically dedicated to the man's ancestral spirits and indicated that the man felt that Christianity was a direct threat to his way of life.

If, on the other hand, a spiritualist likes the missionary or sees some possibility of forming a relationship that could bring some gain, then outright rejection is unlikely. Now the possible responses range from a fake or shallow acceptance of the missionary's message to a deep conversion.

Why would a spiritualist fake a conversion? This worldview is all about manipulating spirits for one's personal advantage, and it does not normally envisage worship of the Supreme Being. The Creator God is seen as distant and unconcerned with humans, whereas multitudes of lesser spirits intervene in human life regularly. Veneration of ancestral spirits is done in order to receive their blessings; consulting the *inyanga* is done to determine which spirit is bringing bad luck or calamity in order to appease it or block its activity through the use of fetishes or charms. In either case, the center of this religious activity is human need, and everything is done to get the spirits either working for humans or at least neutralized so they do no harm.

This does not mean that spiritualists can become confident in their manipulation. Spirits are too numerous, powerful, and capricious for that. Generally, the attitude spiritualists have toward the spirit world is one of fear and resignation, realizing that the forces arrayed against them are so superior that their best efforts to channel the spirits' activity are probably not good enough. Fatalism describes this resignation to personal lack of control. Whatever will be will be.

Since the spiritualist feels somewhat helpless, like a person trying to restrain the ocean's waves that would toss one about, he or she usually tries to cover all the bases in order to get some protection. When Jesus is presented as a powerful person, the Son of God, who can perform miracles, the spiritualist would like such a person as guardian. Spiritualists like rituals, so when the evangelist explains the rite of baptism, the spiritualist is only too happy to take advantage of it. For the spiritualist, baptism has a magical quality, as rituals performed by the *inyanga* do, but there may not be much personal commitment to Jesus involved.

At the center of the spiritualist's worldview is the preservation of the self in one's ancient community. In one sense, this is the essence of any worldview, since cultural assumptions are usually based on the preservation of a way of life. The key distinction for the spiritualist is that a person sees himself or herself as part of an entire web of being stretching from the Creator through the ancestral spirits and on into the visible world of family and property. The self's identity comes from that web of being, so that a person cannot see himself or herself apart from it. It is more than just identity that one receives, for an African perceives that his or her life force comes from belonging to this web.

When I was in the Peace Corps in Zaire (now called the Democratic Republic of the Congo) in the early 1970s, I came across an important book called *Bantu Philosophy* by Placide Tempels. Tempels was a Catholic missionary in Zaire and had studied the worldview of the Baluba people in depth. As a young Peace Corps volunteer, I found myself also living among the Baluba in central Zaire. No one at the time was talking in terms of the Bantu (Africans) having any philosophy, so the book caught my attention and I absorbed Tempels's description of how Africans think. Now after several decades of living among various African peoples, I still think Tempels described their worldview most clearly.

Tempels coined the term "life force" or "vital force" as the unique aspect of Bantu philosophy, which of course was not written down in books but is experiential and observable. Here is how Tempels described the person who believes in vital force:

> The Bantu cannot be a lone being. It is not a good enough synonym for that to say he is a social being. No; he feels and knows himself to be a vital force, at this very time to be in intimate and personal relationship with other forces acting above him and below him in the hierarchy of forces. He knows himself to be a vital force, even now influencing some forces and being influenced by others. The human being, apart from the ontological hierarchy and the interaction of forces, has no existence in the conceptions of the Bantu.[1]

Another experience I had in the Emakhandeni suburb illustrates what Tempels is saying. Elliot Donga and I were evangelizing door-to-door and met a dedicated spiritualist named Sibanda. I still remember his clan name because he emphasized it so strongly. Ndebele people belong to a limited number of clans and Sibanda is a common one. After Elliot and I had carefully explained the gospel and how to become a Christian, Sibanda replied, "I am Sibanda. My father is Sibanda and my grandfather is Sibanda. My ancestors are Sibanda. If I become a Christian, are you saying that I will have to give up honoring my ancestors?" Clearly Sibanda could not conceive of his existence apart from his clan, whether living or dead. When I explained about the lordship of Jesus in all things for a Christian, Sibanda said he would like to become a Christian, but not on such terms.

1. Tempels, *Bantu Philosophy*, 103–4.

Who Needs a Missionary?

Most shallow conversions of spiritualists come from accepting Jesus as Savior but not as Lord. This is also true of secular people, but for spiritualists, the difference is that they must displace whatever spirits lie in control of the self at the heart of their worldview in favor of the Lord Jesus. This means in essence that one must lay down all attempts to manipulate the spirit world in one's favor, letting Jesus rule in the heart. Gailyn van Rheenen said, "Christian conversion is the enthroning of Christ at the center of a person's life and allowing him to control every aspect of it."[2] Perhaps ancestral spirits allow people to manipulate the spirit realm, but Jesus does not. For everyone, self must be dethroned to place Jesus in his rightful place as king of our lives.

What is the actual meaning of the heart of a worldview? If we conceive of a worldview as made up of layers like an onion, the heart of the worldview is the deepest level of the self and hence is the real aim of conversion. Van Rheenen stated, "Christian conversion without worldview change in reality is syncretism."[3] So how do we understand worldview? Paul Hiebert has a diagram of the elements of worldview in his important book *Anthropological Insights for Missionaries*.[4] Worldviews are basic assumptions about reality that lie at the heart of any culture and find themselves bearing fruit in all aspects of culture such as social structure, education, laws, politics, economics, and religion. They directly affect our ways of knowing, our feelings and emotions, and our judgments and evaluations.

A book that has helped me understand this way of analyzing a worldview is David Burnett's *Clash of Worlds*. Burnett explains worldview as the underlying framework that supports a culture, much as the trunk of a tree and its branches support the leaves.[5] Often the observer notes immediately the abundance of foliage but not the underlying branches. So it is with cultures. A casual observer who first arrives in a place notices the sights, sounds, and smells, comparing them automatically with the place he or she came from. Frequently, the new arrival then makes judgments based on the familiar, wrongly assuming that the rules governing his or her own worldview apply in the new situation as well. This naturally tilts the observer's evaluation of the new culture toward the negative. A thorough evaluation

---

2. Van Rheenen, *Communicating Christ*, 88.
3. Ibid., 89.
4. Hiebert, *Anthropological Insights*, 46.
5. Burnett, *Clash of Worlds*, 13.

Conversion

of a culture, however, will involve an understanding of its worldview in depth.

In terms of worldview, then, how do we define conversion? We can look at it as a worldview shift[6] or a paradigm shift.[7] This kind of definition would seem to encompass all types of conversion, shallow or deep. A paradigm shift especially signifies a new way of thinking such as scientists have when a major new discovery is made. For example, Einstein's Theory of Relativity changed the way scientists had thought about physics since the time of Isaac Newton. Paradigm and worldview shifts are new ways of thinking, and certainly this is involved in conversion, but such terms seem inadequate to encompass a deep conversion to Christ on the order of what Isaac experienced.

Paul Hiebert went further with his description of conversion in a later book, *Transforming Worldviews*, saying, "Conversion to Christ must encompass all three levels of culture: behavior and rituals, beliefs, and worldview. Christians should live differently because they are Christians."[8] He regarded worldview as the deepest level that is often untouched in shallow conversions. If conversion remains at the level of behavior, ritual, or even belief, it runs the risk of being held captive to the convert's original culture. "The result is syncretistic Christo-paganism, which has the form but not the essence of Christianity. Christianity becomes a new form of magic and a new, more subtle form of idolatry."[9] He concluded, "Transforming worldviews must be central to church and mission in the twenty-first century."[10]

Scripture describes such a conversion as being "born again," or "born from above." Jesus told Nicodemus that even a person like him, a trained religious leader, must be born again: "I tell you the truth, no one can see the kingdom of God unless he is born again" (John 3:3). Whatever is the full meaning of "born again," it involves the supernatural work of the Holy Spirit, as Jesus explained to Nicodemus: "Flesh gives birth to flesh, but the Spirit gives birth to spirit" (John 3:6). Whereas worldview and paradigm shifts are happening all the time as people become convinced that one way of thinking is better than another, deep conversion to Jesus Christ is only the work of the Holy Spirit.

6. Hiebert, *Anthropological Insights*, 49.
7. Burnett, *Clash of Worlds*, 222.
8. Hiebert, *Transforming Worldviews*, 315.
9. Ibid.
10. Ibid.

Who Needs a Missionary?

In one sense at least, it is impossible to be a true follower of Jesus Christ without a miracle happening in your life. This goes very much against the thinking of a person from a secular background, but it is biblical. Paul explains that Christians differ from non-Christians at this point: the possession of the Holy Spirit who interprets reality. "We have not received the spirit of the world but the Spirit who is from God, that we may understand what God has freely given us" (1 Cor 2:12). He further says, "The man without the Spirit does not accept the things that come from the Spirit of God, for they are foolishness to him, and he cannot understand them, because they are spiritually discerned" (1 Cor 2:14). Only Christians have the "mind of Christ" (1 Cor 2:16).

Isaac certainly has the mind of Christ, as this book shows. He proved that over several decades. Others that I worked with more closely than with Isaac did not show the mind of Christ so clearly. For some, the reason was that their conversion to Christ was shallow, but for others, the situation resembled that of the Corinthians. In the verse immediately following the one about having the mind of Christ, Paul reprimands them, "Brothers, I could not address you as spiritual but as worldly—mere infants in Christ" (1 Cor 3:1). Obviously, many Christians do not live up to their potential even though they have the Holy Spirit.

Summary

As the parable of the sower indicates, not all people who accept the gospel have the same level of commitment to follow through with its implications (Matt 13:3–9). Conversion may be shallow, as in the case of people whose hearts are described as "rocky places" without deep soil (Matt 13:5), or as ground infested with thorns that stifle the growth of the seed (Matt 13:7). Jesus explained that his illustrations meant that some people allowed trouble, persecution, the cares of life, or the lure of earthly wealth to crowd out the Spirit's work in conversion (Matt 13:21–22). How can we tell whether a person's conversion is deep or shallow? Only time can show that, since Jesus said it is by our fruits that people can recognize what is really in our hearts (Matt 7:16–20), and fruits take time to mature.

Conversion is not simply a worldview change or a paradigm shift, but is a work of God. It needs to happen at the deepest level of our being. The Holy Spirit does a miracle in the heart as he did with Isaac, changing his outlook entirely. Even if the evangelist presents the gospel clearly, the Holy

Spirit must also gain unhindered access to the heart if conversion is to be life changing. Following conversion, each day of a person's life is a walk with God on an adventure of faith that has the potential to produce lasting fruit. Isaac's story will provide plenty of good illustrations of this journey with God. And the next steps of faith should transform a convert into a true disciple, or follower, of Christ.

2

Training

For a new believer in Christ, there is a bewildering variety of Christians to follow. Apart from the usual imported churches of Catholics and Protestants, Zimbabwe also has hundreds of home-grown churches, most of which are known collectively as Zionists. And then there were the Wolhuters, Isaac's bosses, who were in a category all their own.

To illustrate some of the visible differences between various Catholic and Protestant churches first, quite apart from any issues stemming from the Reformation, Africans wanted to know what debatable practices they could keep as members of a particular group. In their minds they divided churches between high and low churches, rather than Catholic or Protestant. We frequently had Africans ask us up front at our first meeting, "If we join your church what do you allow us to do? Will we be able to smoke and drink beer?" I remember one ecumenical Christmas party held at an Anglican Church. As participants from numerous local churches entered the hall, they had to state their church membership and were then assigned seats. It soon became evident that all the churches that allowed alcoholic drinks were seated on one side of the hall and all that opposed such drinking were on the other side. This seating arrangement made serving the drinks more convenient. For the record, most conservative African Protestants do not allow either beer or tobacco. In addition to any scriptural reasons, beer and snuff are often associated with ancestral spirit worship in African traditional religion.

Ancestral spirit worship is another key variable among churches. Roman Catholics and the mainline Protestant denominations that allow alcohol and tobacco also tend to overlook worshipping these spirits on the side.

From the Roman Catholic and Anglican perspective, contacting the spirits seems akin to praying to the saints. In this way many Christians in places like Zimbabwe are two-tier Christians, appearing to resemble Christians from any other part of the planet when in the formal worship services, but secretly or even openly using the services of traditional healers when in some crisis. This habit of mixing two religions is called syncretism.

Most of the Zionist churches that I know about are also syncretistic, but in a very different way from Anglicans or Catholics. While they strongly oppose ancestral spirit worship, they support polygamy and numerous Old Testament laws. The name "Zionist" has little to do with Israel, although like most Christians, they have a fondness for Israel and sing a lot about Jerusalem. The name stems rather from John Alexander Dowie's utopian city of Zion, Illinois and his Pentecostal church that sent missionaries to South Africa in 1904.[1] This resulted not only in some Pentecostal churches being planted there, but also in an unforeseen explosion of Zionist churches all over southern Africa. Wherever Christianity has spread, it has had the unintended consequence of spawning all sorts of fringe movements in addition to what we would consider orthodox ones.

Because of their heritage, Zionists look and act like Pentecostals. This is why they attack ancestral spirit worship, now seen as idolatrous. On the other hand, they are syncretistic in retaining other elements of African traditional religion while adding some characteristically Jewish traditions. For example, they allow men to marry several wives as this was permitted both in African tradition and in Old Testament law. In addition, they forbid the eating of the unclean foods listed in Leviticus 11, like pig meat or *mophane* worms (a caterpillar that lives in the *mophane* tree, considered a delicacy by most traditional Africans). They take the example of Moses at the burning bush in Exodus 3 as prescriptive for today's worship; therefore they also take off their shoes when on the holy ground of their places of worship, which are often conducted outdoors. Many of them dress like Moses, or what they imagine Moses looked like, with white robes and a shepherd's staff in their hand.

A central issue for Zionists and other such African Initiated Churches (AICs) is the role of prophecy. Significant time in each worship service is given to prophetic utterances regarding personal issues of the membership. Certain leaders are recognized as having the role of prophet and these often preach to the whole congregation and prophesy to members perceived as having problems. In some ways, they take the same role as traditional

---

1. Daneel, *Quest for Belonging*, 54.

Who Needs a Missionary?

healers by pointing out problems and solutions for spiritual issues. They quite naturally operate in an African frame of reference.

We once had a visitor from Memphis, Tennessee who arrived in Bulawayo on a Sunday afternoon and asked to attend an African worship service. Since the ones I normally attended were already over, I took him to the Bulawayo Baptist Church evening service at 6:00 pm. Although the young people who attended were mostly African, the service was in English and the worship songs were familiar to the visitor. When the service ended, our visitor expressed disappointment: "I flew in from my business trip to South Africa hoping to catch some authentic African worship, but that service could have been done in Memphis." As he had to resume his business matters in South Africa the next day, he requested that we find another African service.

Then I thought of our farm church led by Tennyson Todd that met on a white-owned farm near Esigodini. As the farm workers had to work all day on Sunday, they met for worship only around 8:00 pm after they had bathed and eaten dinner. What I didn't know was that the farm foreman had forced the Zionist workers to meet with our church that day. He was trying to control the Zionist activities that arose from night meetings outdoors on the farm, such as ecstatic dances that sometimes led to unwanted pregnancies. He wrongly assumed that forcing them to combine with our group would make them more conventional Christians.

We arrived at the farm just as both groups were entering the abandoned farm house where our church met. Immediately we could see that the Zionists were there by their white and green apparel with a cross emblazoned on the back. As we entered worship, it wasn't long before the Zionist leader began rolling his head from side to side and then uttered a long "Creeeeeeeee! A thousand miles to heaven!" As he was sitting next to the man from Memphis, I felt I had to whisper some explanation: "That's the prophet!"

The Zionists were not deterred by being placed under our church leader, Tennyson, and their prophet tried to take over the service. After Tennyson preached, the prophet preached even longer and louder. After the sermons, Tennyson did what I had become accustomed to. He invited sick people to come forward, asked them what ailed them, then laid hands on them and prayed. One woman carried a sick baby to Tennyson, who took the child in his hands and prayed for its healing. Almost all the African services I have attended in Zimbabwe, a country with limited medical care, conclude with individual prayers for the sick. The Zionist prophet mirrored most of what Tennyson did, except that he did not ask anyone what was wrong, appearing to know that already. Then he did something unexpected. A Zionist woman came up carrying a parcel that she handed to the prophet. He unwrapped the parcel, which contained several red candles. He proceeded to pray for the candles held in his hands, just as Tennyson had prayed for the baby. Our friend from Memphis asked me what was going on, but I said I had no idea as this was new to me too.

When the service was over, I asked about the meaning of the prayer for the candles and got this explanation: the woman was asking the prophet to bless the candles so that when she lit them in her house, the flames would spread blessings to all who lived there. I told our visitor that he had seen some things that numerous missionaries had not seen even after years of living in Africa. Not only had he witnessed the prayer for candles, a first for me, but he had also seen a person with a manifestation of a demon. Both Tennyson and the Zionist offered fervent prayer for the demonized person, but again the prophet was much more charismatic. Hoping our American friend had not been offended by all this strange new behavior, I asked him what he thought of the service. "That was some African worship service, alright!" he replied.

On another occasion, I was visiting a new church that our evangelist, Johnson Maphosa, had planted at a farm run by ARDA, the Agriculture and Rural Development Authority, at Mphoengs on the Botswana border. ARDA is a parastatal organization that has farms around the country. This one provided irrigation for winter wheat in a particularly arid part of Zimbabwe. It was winter time and the temperature often got down to freezing at night in this location. Our new converts were again farm workers who could only meet after dark on Sundays. The ARDA workers were provided with tiny houses into which we crammed so many people for worship services that there was standing room only. Being packed in like sardines helped to raise the temperature in the room, but made it very hard to sit down.

Meanwhile outside, the Zionist farm workers were just starting their worship service as we were dismissing ours. In this part of Zimbabwe, Zionism is regarded as standard Christianity, and people here often react negatively to what we see as orthodox Christianity. On both sides of the border with Botswana live the Kalanga people, and for some reason Zionism is rampant among them. There are probably hundreds of different Zionist churches along the border, as they keep splitting in order to follow their preferred prophet. Their church names reflect their creativity: The

Who Needs a Missionary?

New Holyfull [*sic*] Gospel Apostolic Church of God in Zion, The Spiritual Healing Church, or The African Collar Church, known for the wide green collars in its uniform.

On this particular night, I got an indelible image in my mind of what Zionist worship is like. Night services in rural Zimbabwe are always dimly lit by candles or kerosene lamps, which often lend them an eerie glow. Most African worship is exuberant, but the Zionists take it to a new level. They like to dance in circles and on that night they became like whirling dervishes. Their singing and dancing in a circle, with each dancer spinning round and round, robes swirling in the dim light, created a surreal scene. Faster and faster they spun as the singing intensified. The scene was nothing short of mesmerizing. Zionists always put an incredible amount of energy into their worship, and frequently hold all night prayer meetings in the bush.

As we think about how Isaac grew in his new faith, he had many such expressions of Christianity to choose from, all as different as chalk and cheese. Initially, he started attending our Famona Disciples of Christ Church with Sandy Wolhuter and her children. That is where he began worshipping with my wife and me along with our colleagues, Allen and Janelle Avery. But the worship at this church was in English at that stage, and although Isaac could understand it fairly well, he could not speak it and does not use English much to this day. Furthermore, the worship style appealed to European tastes, as white people made up the majority of the membership in those early days. For most Africans, white worship is unbearably sedate, and they will not go for it unless compelled by some missionary who insists that it is the right way to worship God.

Three decades later I returned to Famona for a Sunday worship service after living in the USA for some time. I found that many things in the church had not changed one bit in all those years: the same books were in the bookcase by the entrance, the same photos on the bulletin board, the same banners on the sanctuary wall, the same furniture in the same arrangement, and even some of the same people were there. But when it came to worship, everything had changed. The children that Mari-Etta had taught in Sunday School now led worship as a large praise team with upbeat music sung in various African and European languages (including Portuguese!). The leaders took turns leading, accompanied by vigorous keyboard playing, with much swaying and pivoting of bodies. And it went on for about forty-five minutes. In honor of my presence, the master of ceremonies went into the "office" to retrieve copies of the English chorus book that the Averys had published. He asked me to choose a couple of choruses for old times' sake and we sang "As the deer panteth for the water" and "In moments like these, I lift up my hands" with gusto!

As a body, the Famona group did not impact Isaac all that much. Instead his personal spiritual growth began with Sandy Wolhuter, who like her husband, tended to march to a different beat. The first thing Sandy did was to allow Isaac time off on Sunday mornings to go to the Famona Church, in addition to his regular day off each week. Then she invited Isaac into her house each Monday evening for prayers together. It was highly unusual for a boss to invite a worker inside the house for any reason; Sandy even served tea after they had prayed.

Geoff was not yet a Christian, and this deeply concerned Sandy. During the Monday evening prayers with Isaac, Geoff would withdraw to the bedroom, leaving Sandy and Isaac to pray for him specifically. Both Geoff's father and brother had died in motorcycle accidents, and Sandy was worried about Geoff's continued infatuation with his motorcycle. In fact, he had registered to enter a motorbike race and had already paid the entrance fee. During the low level guerrilla war in Zimbabwe before independence, Geoff was part of a motorcycle platoon that patrolled the Matopos Hills south of their chicken farm. When they came under fire from guerrillas in the rocky hills, his platoon would dive off their bikes, take cover in the bush, and return fire. Geoff loved this kind of action and doing it on his motorbike was icing on the cake.

Sandy asked Isaac to pray that Geoff would stop entering such races. Amazingly, Geoff ended up not participating in the race, which both Sandy and Isaac took as a direct answer to their fervent prayers. I remember the day that Geoff came to tell Allen Avery that he was ready to become a Christian. In addition to being a chicken farmer, which was never that profitable, Geoff was also a printer for the main Bulawayo daily newspaper, *The Chronicle*. He continued to ride his motorbike to work and that day he had an accident on the way. He was thrown from his motorcycle and went sliding along the highway, receiving numerous cuts and abrasions. He showed up at Allen's house a bit black and blue from his injuries, and he simply stated, "I'm ready to join the team." After that Geoff was just as sincere a Christian as Sandy.

What I had not realized at the time was the role Isaac played in Geoff's conversion. When Geoff was deciding whether to become a Christian, he called in Isaac and spoke to him through a translator named Ncube, a farm worker colleague of Isaac. Geoff did an amazing thing: as Isaac's boss he knelt in front of him and asked him to lay his hands on him and pray for him as he was now ready to believe in Jesus as his own Lord and Savior. This preceded his motorcycle accident on the way to work and his subsequent visit to tell Allen Avery that he was ready to become a Christian. All these years I had not known this part of the sequence of events that brought Geoff to faith.

Isaac's ability to minister began to show up in other ways too. The Wolhuters' maid, Lina Mpofu, began to complain about having to wash Isaac's teacups from the Monday night prayers. But more than that, she was jealous of Isaac's growing influence on the Wolhuters. Her mother was an *inyanga*, and Lina believed that the way to gain power and influence—or to undermine the influence of someone you were jealous of—was through the ancestral spirits, called *amadlozi*.

To provide some background on Lina's involvement in occultic practices, a visit to our home in Esigodini by her mother, MaSibanda, offers some clues. MaSibanda was wearing the bead necklaces called *ubuhlalu* that identify an *inyanga*. By that time in my culture study, I knew enough to be able to recognize the beads as significant. We were having the customary cup of tea with MaSibanda and another African woman, Esnathi Moyo, who occasionally worked for us. While sipping our tea, I asked a question about ancestral spirits: "Why is it that grandparents, who are usually kind to their grandchildren when they are alive, will strike them with illness when they become spirits?" Any form of chronic illness that resists western medical treatment can be a sign that the *amadlozi* want to communicate with their living offspring. The family would call in an *inyanga* to diagnose the illness and prescribe a cure. This usually involved brewing beer, dancing all night, and having someone become a medium for the spirit who could convey the spirits' message to the family.

When I posed that question to MaSibanda, she didn't reply at all; rather, she slowly reacted by belching twice from the depths of her stomach. This apparently had nothing to do with the tea she had been consuming, but everything to do with communicating with the spirits. Esnathi became a ghastly ashen color when MaSibanda belched, and gasped, "Don't ask her any more questions! Don't ask her any more questions!" Like a referee in a boxing match, Esnathi was determined to separate MaSibanda and me for my own safety. She was deeply afraid of MaSibanda's power that seemed to be threatening to erupt. I realized that African traditional religion is based on deep-seated fears that can be exploited at will. Our conversation ended there and we had little contact with MaSibanda after that.

Isaac was familiar with that whole African traditional worldview, which he had recently left behind, but it no longer frightened him as it did Esnathi. One Monday night, Sandy held the evening prayers in the communal kitchen next to the farm workers' quarters. This time Geoff and their children also attended. During the time of worship, Lina began to lead a song entitled, "*Igazi likaJesu Lodwa*," a translation of the English hymn "Nothing but the Blood of Jesus." While singing, Lina suddenly fell over in a dead faint. Sandy rushed to help her and asked Geoff to take her immediately in their car to the Esigodini hospital. But Isaac simply said, "Let's pray for her," knowing it had to do with Lina's *amadlozi*.

So he laid hands on her and prayed for her deliverance from the spirits. Lina cried out loudly while the Wolhuters looked on with concern. To their astonishment, she returned to her senses and sat up. From that point on, Lina complained that Isaac had diminished her spiritual power by expelling her ancestral spirits. Casting out a demon seemed to come second-nature to him, whereas it presented a considerable problem for a Western missionary like me, for whom it was uncharted territory. The Wolhuters were beginning to realize that Isaac was going to be a valuable gospel minister.

Sandy began to encourage Isaac to use his Christian gifts more and more. She first took him around the neighboring white-owned farms in the evenings after work to preach to her own friends, who sometimes referred Isaac to their farm workers instead. If Isaac was sent to the workers' compound, Sandy would join him there for the evening outreach. In order to maintain this level of evangelism, the Wolhuters reduced his farm work to sixteen days per month while keeping his wages at about the same level. This allowed him time to study his Bible.

Realizing Isaac's strong effort to receive training and indeed to train others in the Christian life, I began to record a series of lessons on basic discipleship for him and others to listen to on audio cassettes. From a South African group named CAVA (Christian Audio-Visual Action), who specialized in supplying material and equipment for such training, we obtained several hand-cranked tape recorders. They could be used anywhere with no need for electricity or batteries. We spread these around the growing number of churches that our team planted in Matabeleland so leaders in each district could listen to cassette tapes and learn while remaining in their places of residence, active in God's work.

Who Needs a Missionary?

The standing joke soon got to be about the way I opened each lesson with "*NginguKhumalo okhulumayo*," meaning "This is Khumalo speaking." In Ndebele this sounds quite lyrical. A Malawian church member named Sibanda who was also a drunkard gave me the name Khumalo. When we first arrived in Zimbabwe, we were given a church to shepherd by its founder, a Malawian named Mkandawire, who had decided to return to his homeland. We had not intended to dive into church work so soon, before we adequately learned Ndebele, but it was something of a crisis that Mkandawire had to leave just then, at the time when he had just launched a new work. So he bequeathed to us a ragtag group of squatters who met for Sunday service under a tree on the outskirts of Bulawayo at a squatter camp known as Two Stamp, named after the worked-out mine where it was located near the suburb of Killarney.

Most of the squatters were Malawians, so their Ndebele was a bit limited. We had to use our time at Two Stamp as a language learning opportunity, since our language learning had not gone far. Apparently my own careful study of Ndebele caused this one old Malawian in our new church to call me Khumalo, which is the clan of the royal family, the true Ndebele speakers. The name stuck and our church members still call me that today, even though Sibanda was drunk when he said it. When startled Zimbabweans first hear them use that name for me, I simply explain that I am a child of King Jesus. Hence I gladly opened each tape lesson with "*NginguKhumalo okhulumayo*."

Isaac listens to a tape played on a hand-cranked recorder.

With Isaac, I can't honestly say that the taped lessons were essential for his growth. He learned by doing, so sitting and turning a tape recorder was helpful only up to a point. Isaac knew that he needed to know the Scriptures better, but he was a poor reader, so the tapes helped in that way. Still he needed more. He needed to become even more active in God's work to learn hands-on how to win people and how to form churches (which the tapes talked about), but also how to win spiritual battles with Satan.

As Isaac moved closer to his goal of becoming an evangelist, we sent him out with a Foxfire team to evangelize villages in the Esigodini area. Foxfire was a ministry of African Enterprise, a South African parachurch organization that we had worked with in a city-wide crusade in Bulawayo. The name "Foxfire" came from the destructive little experiment that Samson conducted among the Philistines, seeing how much grain he could burn down by tying foxes' tails together and then setting them on fire (Judg 15:3–5). This African Enterprise outreach was apparently designed to set the rural areas of Zimbabwe on fire with the gospel in a direct challenge to Satan over his undisputed territory.

Isaac joined a team of two other men, Sibanda and Phiri, who worked for Foxfire under the field supervision of a man named Dlamini. Dlamini instructed them to stay with non-Christians in village homes and to record everything they saw going on in that home. There was plenty to record, such as the distilling of potent moonshine called *itototo*. Each day they conducted an evangelistic outreach to the surrounding houses and then returned to the home where they were staying to spend time teaching their hosts. Seven days a week, then, the group of three men lived and worked among non-Christians, which brought with it numerous temptations.

One day, after a hard day of evangelizing, they returned to the place they were sleeping to find that each man had a girl in his sleeping bag, waiting for him. These were girls from the homes they had been evangelizing. Even at the village of New Line, where Isaac had become a church leader in a new church we helped to plant, temptations abounded. Non-Christian women there sent three girls to eat with the three men and to tempt them sexually. Eventually, the men became so jaded by all this that they withdrew from the villages to take refuge at a rest camp next to the Wolhuters's farm, where they spent some time fasting, drinking only tea for seven days.

Isaac said he learned several things from the three months and three weeks that he spent with Foxfire. First, he found the courage to enter non-Christian homes to share the gospel. Second, he learned how to face and withstand sexual temptation (I recall that one of the Foxfire men was later accused of impregnating a girl in the one of the Esigodini villages). Third, he learned how to fast for spiritual battles. And fourth, he observed all kinds of non-Christian practices, some of which he had never seen before.

For example, one home forbade the use of salt on food, which is considered an absolute necessity by many Africans. The reason was that this family used salt for magical purposes only, sprinkling it liberally around the yard to ward off evil spirits. Another family possessed a secret room into which only the head of the home could enter. One day, the Foxfire team prayed about how to gain access to this room to see what was going on inside. They then followed the man of the house into the room when he went in, to find it full of items dedicated to witchcraft, such as a headdress made from a horse tail. The man explained to them that these items gave him power over his enemies. The Foxfire team touched and handled some of the items and asked to be allowed to take some to show Dlamini.

From such raw experiences, Isaac learned to function as a Christian evangelist in a hostile environment without fear. He was well aware of human weakness, including his own, but was prepared to continue his work regardless. Most likely, he learned some of that attitude from his boss, Geoff, who could be both hot-tempered and forgiving after he became a Christian. There was often tension between Geoff, a former Rhodesian army fighter, and a neighboring farmer, Samani, who fought on the side of the opposing guerrilla forces. The tension rose to a boiling point when Samani's cattle kept coming into Geoff's fields just as crops were ripening. After warning Samani four times to keep his cattle from eating his crops, Geoff took matters into his own hands.

One evening, he entered the field where the cattle were busy destroying his crops and gunned down six of them with an automatic weapon. He proceeded to tell the police what he had done, reminding them that he had repeatedly informed them about the offending cattle each time he had warned Samani. The police brought Samani to Geoff's farm to see his dead cattle, but he became furious and refused to remove the carcasses, referring the matter to the courts. Geoff had no alternative but to slaughter the cattle himself and sell the beef.

On the court date, Geoff asked Isaac to pray hard before he went to face the judge. Later that day, Geoff returned shouting, "Hallelujah!" The judge had surprisingly not only found him not guilty, but allowed him to keep all the money from the sale of the beef and fined Samani all the court costs. Geoff, on the other hand, had no intention of keeping the funds for himself. He told Isaac that they should both pay a visit to Samani in order to return the money. Aware that the meeting might not be friendly, Geoff armed himself and gave Isaac a pistol, and they prayed they wouldn't need to use them.

When they got to the gate, Samani saw them and turned to go into his house where he armed himself. His wife opened the gate and let the vehicle in. She let Geoff and Isaac into the house, both carrying concealed pistols, as they came face to face with Samani. Geoff surprised Samani by apologizing for the whole episode of the cattle slaughter and offering him the money from the sale of the beef. They shook hands and both signed a peace pact before Geoff and Isaac left, rejoicing at the positive outcome and praying a prayer of thanksgiving in the truck before they went home.

In case you are wondering what Isaac might have done if Samani had come out of his room with guns blazing, Geoff had given Isaac some solid training in using a firearm. This arose not with Samani in mind at all. It came about some years earlier when dissident activity in the Esigodini area was increasing. "Dissidents" was the term used for former guerrilla fighters from Matabeleland who were locked out of power by the guerrilla faction that won the first universal election in Zimbabwe in 1980. These disgruntled fighters refused to lay down their weapons and went on sporadic shooting sprees in Matabeleland, often targeting white farmers.

Geoff was prepared for any possible attack, but when he and his family wished to leave the farm for a vacation, he decided it was time to train his most trusted worker how to use a firearm. He took him for target practice to rifle ranges and then supplied him with an FN rifle that was standard issue in the Rhodesian army. His instructions to Isaac for the time his family would be away on vacation were that Isaac should sleep inside the main house with the FN close at hand. If anyone should knock on the door during the night, Isaac was not to open it, but to slip out of the window and sneak around the outside of the house to see who it was. If it was someone he didn't know, he was to shoot first and ask questions later.

When the Wolhuters left, Isaac spent night after uneventful night sleeping alone in their house. Finally, one night, there came a knock at the door. As instructed, Isaac silently picked up his FN rifle and stepped out the window. As he peered through the darkness, he spotted Sandy Wolhuter in the family car with the children, while Geoff was knocking on the door. Silently he slipped up to Geoff and tapped him on the shoulder, startling him. When he realized it was Isaac carrying the FN, he relaxed and said, "Good job, Isaac!" Such was life with the Wolhuters.

Now Isaac was preparing to move on to a new and more challenging phase of his life. His initial training was coming to an end and now the real work was about to begin. He had decided to return to his home village near Siabuwa in Binga District to preach the gospel and plant a church if there were any converts. Before he left the Wolhuters, he had a serious conversation with one of his own converts from a neighboring farm, a man named German Dube. German was from a rough background, a traditional African from a family steeped in witchcraft. When Isaac told him that he was about to leave to preach back home, German wanted to know more, because his own home in the Matopos Hills also needed the gospel.

Isaac placed his hands on German and commissioned him to go and plant a church in Gwandavale, in the Matopos. He instructed him, "When you arrive in Gwandavale, show the people that know you how you have thoroughly repented by your own actions." German went to Gwandavale and reported back to Isaac after that first visit, saying he had managed to witness to a few neighbors near his family home. Isaac replied that even a few is fine if they believe the message of salvation in Jesus. Sure enough, the men to whom German began to witness, Robie and Swarnet Ncube, became strong Christian leaders in a new church in Gwandavale. While the older man, Robie, has passed away, Swarnet continues to lead a growing church, and he and his followers have planted several other churches in the Matopos area.

The Necessity of Training

The Great Commission in Matthew 28:19-20 makes it imperative to make disciples of all nations. Much evangelical mission work has done quite well making converts, but has often failed abysmally to make real disciples. Evangelists will roll into town and preach fiery sermons for a week or two, getting lots of responses, only to roll right out of town again. In Zimbabwe, we called that "baby dumping." Sadly, the phenomenon of actual baby dumping became an epidemic in newly independent Zimbabwe. For a variety of reasons, largely economic, young mothers would give birth to healthy babies only to place them in street gutters, flush them down toilets, or put them in trash cans. Some were placed by the road to be picked up by strangers or die.

Training

One of our best evangelists, Samson Mkwananzi, had a background of living on the street and eating out of trash bins. One day, he noticed a young woman coming out of an apartment building and placing a melon-sized parcel wrapped in a plastic bag in the trash can. Assuming that it was leftover *isitshwala* (stiff cornmeal paste that is the standard diet in Zimbabwe) being thrown away, he thought it was his lucky day and went over to retrieve the parcel. Inside he found the lifeless body of a newborn baby. This shocked him to the core of his being and ended up being a factor in his becoming a Christian.

It is no exaggeration to say that the same thing happens when we lead people to Christ and then leave them alone as new babes. They are literally dumped as if they can grow up alone. For many of our missions, the goal appears to be baptism only, without the rest of the Great Commission, "teaching them to obey everything I have commanded you." If we fail to make disciples of new converts, we leave people and churches crippled or worse, dying. How many times have we heard that Christianity in a certain place is "a mile wide and an inch deep"? That is a symptom of spiritual "baby dumping," the practice of letting immature Christians remain that way.

We found that it is important for new converts to get to work immediately, sharing their testimony with non-Christians and getting trained in evangelism while they still have mostly non-Christian friends. New converts are often the best evangelists, because they need only articulate what changes Christ has brought into their lives, backed up by a new character that is visible to those who know them. That is what happened to Samson Mkwananzi. He was converted while eating a plate of *isitshwala* at a soup kitchen for street people in Main Street Methodist Church in Bulawayo as he listened to Fibion Nyevhe, one of our evangelists, preach the gospel. Fibion was about twenty years old while Samson was about forty, so it must have been God's Spirit that took over, since it is not customary in Africa for a younger man to influence an older one in that way.

As soon as Samson was baptized, he disappeared for a couple of months, so I assumed he had reverted quickly to his old street life. However, he soon reappeared, saying that he had started a church in his home area of Nkayi, a hundred miles north of Bulawayo! He had been witnessing what he knew of the gospel to his neighbors. When we went to investigate his claims, we found over a hundred people gathered to meet us, expecting to hear the gospel. Many of them were adult men who are usually the last to accept any new beliefs. We began to ask them why they were interested in the gospel, and the consistent answer was that they had seen such a remarkable change in Samson that they wanted what he had! And that is also what his own wife said to us!

Needless to say, we knew it would be important to train Samson as quickly as we could, because he was already an effective evangelist straight out of the baptismal pool. He proved hard to keep up with, as he continued his evangelistic forays in wider and wider circles, all with the same positive outcomes. He soon became the most prolific church planter we ever had, but his training lagged behind, and soon it became obvious that many of his converts were not being properly grounded in the faith. Training is vital for healthy church growth.

According to Acts 8:1, the persecution following Stephen's death scattered young believers throughout Judea and Samaria. The apostles, however, were not affected by this exodus and remained in Jerusalem for the time being. That meant that newer and less experienced converts were now on their own, many of them for the first time. How did they fare? Acts 8:4 says, "Those who had been scattered preached the word wherever they went." How were they able to do so? The obvious answer is that they had already been trained by their leaders in Jerusalem, so their forced uprooting only served to spread Christianity.

The apostle Paul makes a good case study of how important immediate training is to future usefulness in God's work. Acts 9 depicts Paul as having very little "down time" after his conversion. For three days he was fasting and praying, unable to do much at all after being blinded by Jesus on his way to arrest Christians in Damascus. Then Ananias helped restore his sight and baptized him. Acts 9:20 shows that Paul wasted no time diving into ministry: "At once he began to preach in the synagogues that Jesus is the Son of God." God had predicted to Ananias that Paul would prove useful, and so he was.

By Acts 9:26, Paul had made his way back to Jerusalem, no longer as an emissary of the high priest to make life miserable for Christians, but as a strong evangelist for Christ. Local Christians, however, remained unsure of the sincerity of his conversion. At this point, Barnabas stepped in to mentor Paul and to vouch for him as trustworthy and genuine. This mentoring relationship developed further when Barnabas later called Paul to help him disciple new converts in Antioch (Acts 11:25–26). Finally, Barnabas led Paul into cross-cultural missions when the Holy Spirit picked them from

Training

the leadership at Antioch as the ones to send out preaching (Acts 13:2–3). Throughout those years, Barnabas faithfully mentored Paul, recognizing his talents and building him up in ministry. No wonder Barnabas received a name that means "Son of Encouragement" from the apostles (Acts 4:36) long before Paul came along!

But there are intervening years about which Acts does not speak regarding Paul's development as a missionary. For example, Paul stated in Galatians 1:17 that he spent time in Arabia shortly after his conversion in Damascus. "Arabia" does not refer to the modern state of Saudi Arabia, but rather to the area southeast of Damascus known as Nabatean Arabia in the modern state of Jordan.[2] I had always assumed that Paul spent time there studying the Old Testament and contemplating how Jesus as Messiah and Lord had changed his life and message. That assumption was challenged when I read Eckhard Schnabel's *Paul the Missionary*.

Schnabel points out that the standard interpretation of Paul's missionary development has him doing practically nothing between his conversion in AD 31/32 and his first missionary journey with Barnabas in AD 45.[3] Schnabel thinks it "rather unlikely" that Paul would have waited so long before taking seriously Christ's commission for him to be apostle to the Gentiles (Gal 1:15–16). He finds evidence in Galatians 1:16–17; 21–24 that Paul actually undertook a missionary journey from Damascus into Nabatean Arabia, and later another one into Syria and Cilicia.[4]

This theory is supported by Paul's own testimony in Galatians 1 about how he knew from his conversion that he was to be apostle to the Gentiles and how he soon became known in Jerusalem as someone who used to persecute the church but now was preaching Christ. There is no doubt that for Paul, conversion and call to ministry came simultaneously. He stated emphatically while on trial before King Agrippa, "I was not disobedient to the vision from heaven. First to those in Damascus, then to those in Jerusalem and in all Judea, and to the Gentiles also, I preached that they should repent and turn to God" (Acts 26:19–20).

Without Paul's enduring commitment to be an active disciple of Christ, it is doubtful whether Barnabas would have traveled to Tarsus to find him and bring him to Antioch for ministry (Acts 11:25). Would he really have done so if Paul had been sitting around doing nothing during the

2. Schnabel, *Paul the Missionary*, 63–64.
3. Ibid., 40.
4. Ibid.

preceding years? The moral to this story is that those who are converted to Christ also receive a call to ministry that should make them like a racehorse at the starting gate, eager to run down the track that Christ sets for them. In order to run well, they all need training.

A key to the early spread of Christianity was that average Christ followers received such training. Acts 8:1–4 is clear about that, as we have seen. Although the persecution resulting from Stephen's stoning did not affect the apostles, many other Christians scattered out of Jerusalem into Judea and Samaria, spreading the gospel as they went. Ephesians 4:11–12 also confirms that this was not an accident, but was a strategy based on the spiritual gifts of the leaders to equip God's people for all kinds of works of service in order to build and strengthen the body of Christ.

Paul was never without traveling companions, not just to keep from being lonely, but primarily for discipleship. Acts 20:4 gives an impressive list of seven men who were representatives of various churches from the eastern side of the Roman Empire. They were selected by their churches and Paul to help him convey gifts from new churches to the original church in Jerusalem. Certainly all of them (and many more men and women) were actively mentored by Paul for ministry as well.

We used Paul's verse in 2 Timothy 2:2 as a guiding principle of our mission in Zimbabwe: "And the things you have heard me say in the presence of many witnesses entrust to reliable men who will also be qualified to teach others." This represents a chain of disciples, as each one is mentored and then mentors others. In my missionary years in Zimbabwe, I was first mentored by Allen Avery who had been a missionary for ten years in Zambia before I began mission work. Afterwards, I tried never to minister alone. In every act of evangelism or church visits or benevolence one or two other men would be with me. Isaac certainly did this too, as we will see in later chapters, and it made his work strong and enduring.

Today, this essential component of practical training has been lost in many of our churches and mission efforts. It reminds me of how my Bible college, Harding University, recruited a seven-foot tall basketball center while I was there. In the Arkansas conference that Harding competed in, this man looked formidable to all opponents, because no one could match his size. But he was intimidating in appearance only, as he had never been trained to play basketball. Most of the season he simply sat on the bench enjoying a full scholarship; when he actually went on the court, it was soon obvious he didn't know the fundamentals. Similarly, in our churches, people sit in the pews and look good but don't know the basics for lack of training.

Training

The classic book by Robert Coleman, *The Master Plan of Evangelism*, is a reaction to this amazing oversight. He shows from the gospels that Jesus trained only a few faithful people during his short ministry on earth. Although he evangelized in many villages and towns and spoke at mass rallies, Jesus concentrated on just a few actual disciples, primarily the twelve apostles. Coleman stated, "The time which Jesus invested in these few disciples was so much more by comparison to that given to others that it can only be regarded as a deliberate strategy."[5]

The result of that strategy was a seeming dearth of converts by the time Jesus ascended to heaven. Coleman noted that Paul mentions only one group of five hundred to whom Jesus appeared after his resurrection (1 Cor 15:6), and Luke mentions only a hundred twenty who prayed in Jerusalem to receive the Holy Spirit that Jesus had promised (Acts 1:15). Judged strictly by the number of converts visible after his ascension, "Jesus doubtless would not be considered among the most productive mass evangelists of the church."[6] The strategy that Jesus pursued ensured a solid foundation "on which can be built an effective and continuing evangelistic ministry to the multitudes."[7] He concentrated on building a strong chain of discipleship that would perpetuate his ministry into the future. Any weak link in that chain might result in a dead end of reproductive ministry; that link becomes the stem of a vine that could soon wither and die.

Roland Allen looked at the process of training from a slightly different point of view. In his classic book, *Missionary Methods: St. Paul's or Ours?*, he contrasted Paul's methods with mission methods of his day. When Allen wrote about a century ago, colonial methods were in use whereby converts were made dependent on missionaries. Western missionaries assumed that their converts were incapable of doing the kinds of things that we have seen Isaac did. If the person bringing you to faith in Christ has such a low view of your potential, even when regenerated by the Holy Spirit, it is no wonder you don't become a strong disciple. Allen stated, "St. Paul did not go about as a missionary preacher merely to convert individuals: he went to establish churches from which the light might radiate throughout the whole country round. . . . It is the training of the first converts which sets the type for the future."[8] For Allen, the essential element of training was to build confidence

---

5. Coleman, *Master Plan of Evangelism*, 37.
6. Ibid., 28.
7. Ibid., 30.
8. Allen, *Missionary Methods*, 81.

that God would empower the disciples to carry on even in the absence of the missionary. Anything less would result in ineffective and dependent churches, as Allen forcefully asserted:

> If the first converts are taught to depend upon the missionary, if all work, evangelistic, educational, social is concentrated in his hands, the infant community learns to rest passively upon the man from whom they receive their first insight into the Gospel.... Instead of seeking [strength] in the working of the Holy Spirit in themselves, they seek it in the missionary. They put him in the place of Christ, they depend on him.[9]

As a result of his methods, Paul stayed in one location for as short a time as "five or six months and then left behind him a church, not indeed free from the need of guidance, but capable of growth and expansion."[10] Lest we think that Paul's converts must have had some advantage over ours in the way of previous training, Allen reminds us that we actually possess one major advantage today that Paul's converts did not have: the complete Bible usually available in the local language.[11] Despite this disadvantage, Paul managed to leave a core of basic doctrines in the hands of capable leaders whom he expected to guide and teach the local body of Christ.

First Thessalonians gives us a glimpse of those basic doctrines that Paul considered essential. This epistle contains the preliminary teaching that Paul usually delivered orally at each new church, but in the case of the Thessalonians, he was prematurely expelled from town before that phase of teaching could be completed. Roland Allen said, "Now in that epistle [1 Thessalonians] we get an extraordinarily clear and coherent scheme of simple mission-preaching not only implied but definitely expressed."[12] Allen enumerated the following elementary teachings:

1. There is one true and living God.
2. Idolatry is sinful and must be forsaken.
3. The wrath of God is ready to be revealed against pagans and Jews who reject Jesus.
4. Judgment will come suddenly and unexpectedly.

---

9. Ibid.
10. Ibid., 82.
11. Ibid., 85.
12. Ibid., 68.

5. Jesus the Son of God, raised from death, is Savior from God's wrath.
6. All are now invited to enter the kingdom of Jesus.
7. Those who believe and turn to God expect the return of Jesus from heaven to save them.
8. Meanwhile their lives must be pure, useful, and watchful.
9. God gave them the Holy Spirit to help them.[13]

Concerning these nine fundamentals, Allen stated, "they form one connected whole of extraordinary power."[14] He mentioned that taken as a whole these truths were good news indeed for people looking for some comprehensive picture of the world that made sense, for some meaningful understanding of right and wrong, for freedom from capricious spirits, for some moral accountability, for forgiveness, for an antidote to oppression, for power to overcome dire circumstances, for a sense of belonging, and for hope in the future.[15]

Apart from such basic doctrines, each believer also needs to know how to give a personal testimony and share the gospel. We tried to prepare new converts to give testimonies from the beginning, while they still had mostly non-Christian friends and networks. The testimony takes its classic form from the blind man Jesus healed in John 9. When told that his healer must be a sinner (for healing on the Sabbath Day), he didn't really know how to reply, but he said, "One thing I do know. I was blind, but now I see!" (John 9:25). Such a statement was irrefutable because the evidence was obviously in plain view. Of course, the very question caused the blind man to reflect on who Jesus is and eventually he found it necessary to worship him (John 9:38).

The basic form of the testimony lays out how a person was before conversion, a simple statement of accepting Jesus as Lord and Savior, and a description of the change it brought personally. Because it is so personal and presumably some of the folks listening knew the person prior to conversion, the change in the person should speak for itself. At this stage, there is no real explanation about who Jesus is (as with the blind man), since the testimony is meant only to let people see that something powerful has happened for the better and that such a change is freely available to everyone.

13. Ibid.
14. Ibid., 69.
15. Ibid., 69–70.

For that reason, we had to limit the amount of time that new converts dwelled on their previous sinful life, as too many gory details tended to derail the purpose of giving the testimony. The really good news is how the person is now, since accepting Jesus.

In this way, the testimony sets the stage for the full gospel presentation. Here I liked to teach a summary of gospel facts that could be remembered by using the five fingers on one hand. The actual presentation is based on Evangelism Explosion (EE), which the Averys had us all learn at a conference early on in our mission work. I continued to use EE throughout my mission work and beyond because of its effectiveness. The five points provide a track for the memory to include fundamental truths, while allowing for the message to be tailored to the individual's needs, as Jesus did, for example, with the Samaritan woman in John 4.

The thumb is the first finger (Africans count starting with the thumb), representing the gift of eternal life, freely given by God (Eph 2:8–9; Rom 6:23). I asked Africans if they had noticed the difference between how they and white people tried to flag down a ride. Africans tend to wave at the approaching vehicle with a motion that signals the driver to slow down, so the whole arm goes up and down, sometimes vigorously, with the palm of the hand held flat and facing down. Europeans, however, stick up their thumbs and move them back and forth. I asked what the reason is for the different hand motions, and usually my audience has no idea. I replied that while Africans expect to pay something for the ride, Europeans use their thumbs to get a free ride! That is usually news to the Africans, who may be converted to thumbing a lift from then on, but the real point is that the thumb is there to remind them that eternal life is completely free.

The index finger is used for pointing, in this case in accusation of things done wrong in life. The key verse is Romans 3:23, "For all have sinned and fall short of the glory of God." I mention that when pointing at others in accusation, we also have three other fingers pointing back at ourselves, although we prefer not to talk about those. Since Africans learn best from stories, a couple of word pictures help cement the idea that even one sin is too much to allow God to accept a person. The first one I got from Agrippa Dube, who headed up the African conferences on EE in Bulawayo. It draws from village life and describes a scene where a woman is cooking over an open fire outdoors. As she stirs the *isitshwala*, a chicken jumps over the pot and drops in some dung as it flies over. When she notices the drop of dung land in the food, does she simply stir it in and serve it or throw out the *isitshwala*? Most Africans say disgustedly that the whole pot is now ruined by one small bit of dung, and so it is with an otherwise excellent life when one sin enters it.

Agrippa Dube also shared a story about a man who goes outside in the morning to pick a ripe pawpaw (papaya) off a tree for his breakfast, only to find a deadly black mamba wrapped around the fruit. Does he hit the snake and in so doing destroy his pawpaw, or leave it alone, hoping the snake with leave on its own? Most Africans say the snake must be dealt with, even if there is no breakfast left afterwards. And so it is with sin: if God smashes our sin he may also destroy us in the process, but sin must be dealt with.

The third finger is the middle finger, the tallest one when the hand is held up vertically. This represents God, the highest being there is. God is both holy and loving at the same time. He loves us and desires to have us enjoy fellowship with him, but he cannot stand our sins (1 John 4:8; 2 Thess 2:12). This presents a dilemma for us, because we cannot approach God while retaining our sinful lives and we cannot save ourselves. But God in his mercy made a way out by sending Jesus, who is represented by the fourth (ring) finger. Since the ring finger is next to the middle finger, it shows how close Jesus is to God. Here the key verse is Isaiah 53:6, which says, "We all, like sheep, have gone astray, each of us has turned to his own way; and the Lord has laid on him the iniquity of us all."

A helpful visual illustration of the process whereby Jesus took our sin is the following: holding the palm of the left hand up, place an object like a book on it. This represents the self with a load of sin. Hold the right hand high with palm facing down to represent God. God loves us but hates our sin, so if he strikes at our sin he will also destroy us. Then show the right hand coming down to the same level as the left hand, both now with palms up; this represents Jesus descending from heaven to be our Savior. Recite the verse from Isaiah 53:6 as you move the book from the left hand to the right, representing the transfer of sin from us to Jesus on the cross.

Notice that recitation of the key verses is best; every disciple of Jesus should have some verses memorized for use with non-Christians at any time. Since we always carry our hands with us, and they conveniently give us a gospel outline, we should also carry the Bible in our heads for two reasons. If we need to pull out a Bible for something as simple as a gospel presentation, we risk losing our audience whose attention may have shifted elsewhere in the time it takes to locate the verse, or we may frighten our audience by brandishing the Scriptures. Secondly, if Scripture is lodged in our brain, it won't matter where we are when the time comes to use it. We see this principle with Jesus' temptation in the wilderness; he overcame each temptation with a memorized verse (Matt 4:1–11).

We have not yet covered the little finger, which represents our response to the gospel with just a tiny "mustard seed" faith (Matt 17:20). Although small, our faith must robustly trust in Jesus for salvation to the extent that it will show itself in good works (John 3:16; Eph 2:8–10). Here EE uses an effective illustration of two chairs, one representing what I am currently trusting in for my life and one representing Jesus. I sit in the chair representing my current faith as a non-Christian or a weak Christian and I contemplate the empty chair representing Jesus. I wonder whether Jesus will support me or disappoint me when I try to trust him. How will I know for sure if Jesus will do what he says? The only way is to remove myself from my old beliefs to go and sit on the new chair (and here I visually do that). Then I confirm that Jesus is more than adequate for my life and for all that I will entrust to him. This is the beginning of true faith and repentance, as I turn my back on old ways to embrace new life in Christ.

With such fundamental truths mastered and internalized, the new believer is on the road to discipleship, but still needs active mentoring such as Isaac got before he moved back home. Here I see a four-step process, based on how Jesus trained his own disciples. First, they watched Jesus in ministry, that is, they were "with him" (Mark 3:14). Second, they participated in small ways in his ministry. For example, they found five loaves and two fish amongst the crowd that had grown hungry listening to Jesus' teaching. After Jesus multiplied the loaves and fish, the disciples served the multitudes and gathered up leftovers (Mark 6:37–44). Third, he sent them out to preach about repentance on short-term mission trips (Mark 6:7–13). When they returned, they had a debriefing time with Jesus (Mark 6:30). Fourth, he left them on their own in ministry after his resurrection and ascension (Acts 1:8–9). In truth, he made it clear that they would never be alone, as he would send the Holy Spirit to guide them when he had gone (John 14:16–18). Chapter 6 will have more on this four-step process for forming mature disciples in the same way that Jesus did.

Summary

In no case can a new believer become a disciple by sitting either in a church pew or in a classroom. Jesus lived with his disciples for over three years, doing ministry that they could see and participate in. In the same way, Christian discipleship should be an apprenticeship under a master teacher who demonstrates how everything is done. We always tell missionaries to "work themselves out of a job" by training local people in all their skills, but we seldom tell others like elders, pastors, evangelists, deacons, women's leaders, youth leaders, or small group leaders to do the same. Yet all need to do so, because new leaders need to be formed at all times for the maximum health and growth of the body of Christ. No one can become an effective leader without significant mentoring and modeling.

Isaac received just enough mentoring to get going. What he needed most was to see ministry in action, although he also needed training in biblical studies as well. In fact, that is what any productive disciple needs. The Bible is a practical textbook, best learned in actual ministry situations. By integrating Bible studies with Christian action, learning is achieved. Doers of the word are always rewarded with better understanding of the Bible as well as better questions to ask of their mentor. Then the time of mentoring will not be long, and the disciple can move on to his or her personal ministry. In Isaac's case, he would soon begin to plant a church.

3

Church Planting

Isaac's sights were set on preaching in his home area of Magobbo. To get to Magobbo from Bulawayo, one travels towards Victoria Falls through the teak forest known to the Ndebele as *emaguswini* on a wonderful two-lane paved road equally as good as any major US highway. This western side of Zimbabwe is so close to the Kalahari Desert that it is sparsely inhabited; the only small town after a hundred miles is Lupane. Further on, at a nondescript junction known as Cross-Dete, the road to Binga leaves the Falls road to head into a series of steep hills leading down to the Zambezi River escarpment. The river valley is home to the Tonga people, and here the road gets worse and worse as it goes along.

While Isaac almost always made the three-hundred mile trip by bus, I only did this once in 1989. I traveled with a missionary apprentice from the USA named Mark Elefritz and with German Dube, Isaac's disciple. We arrived at Bulawayo's Renkini terminus early in the morning for boarding. Even then the terminus was a beehive of activity, with people clamoring to carry or load your luggage, sell you provisions for the journey, or simply ogling two white men who seemed out of place. We boarded a "chicken" bus operated by Wankie Express for the ten-hour trip. "Chicken" bus refers to the fact that these buses carry just about everything including live chickens if people want them transported. With our own provisions tied to the top of the bus, we set out.

Wankie Express lived up to its name as the driver sped down the highway and the bus careened through the hills like a roller coaster. By the time we reached Binga on the shores of Lake Kariba, the more urban and sophisticated Ndebele people had all disembarked and local Tongas filled the bus. The atmosphere in the bus changed dramatically as the Tongas, a garrulous people, guzzled cartons of local beer and grew louder and louder in animated conversations. With standing room only they chattered and laughed as we bumped along a deteriorating road. The sun was setting as we finally disembarked at Nagangala School, where Isaac's children studied.

We still had a five-mile walk from the school to Isaac's home through the gathering night. Isaac was there to meet us at the bus stop and help us with our luggage. We carried what we could, with the rest remaining in the care of someone who would bring it later in a wheelbarrow. We walked through numerous Tonga villages, each made up of extended families, but were able to see less and less. As we started to cross one field, Isaac signaled for us to stop and be quiet. He stood motionless for a minute, listening intently before he gave us a signal that it was okay to cross. Often, he said, elephants ate crops in this field at night and he didn't want to stumble onto them in the dark. So he had been listening for their characteristic noises: rumbling stomachs and the sounds of cornstalks being plucked and munched. He had quickly reverted to the ways of the bush after his sojourn in Bulawayo and on the chicken farm.

Isaac had left Magobbo in 1974 looking for the bright lights of urban life. By 1987, he was burning with desire to return home to preach the gospel. After becoming a Christian, he had entered into a study of Nehemiah that would form a foundational motif for his own calling. He had left home thinking life in Magobbo was okay, despite the lack of opportunities, but Nehemiah presented a different picture. Isaac discovered that Tonga life was actually life amid the ruins, just as Nehemiah realized that Jerusalem lay in ruins. Primarily it was the people themselves who were in ruins. The sins that burdened Isaac were also the sins of his people: hard drinking, adultery, drugs, and witchcraft. Just as Nehemiah decided to leave his job and go alone to work on the ruins, so Isaac felt he must go alone to begin the rebuilding of his own people.

One of the issues Isaac mentioned as part of his people's ruins may need some extra explanation. The Tongas, like many other African peoples, practice a form of Levirate marriage as described in the Old Testament (Deut 25:5–10). During a visit I paid to Isaac's home in 2010, an elderly Tonga man approached Isaac and me with a sincere plea for help. He was a Christian polygamist, who had probably been allowed to become a church member with all of his wives since he had been a polygamist before conversion. He was a member of another church, and one of his three wives had recently died. According to Tonga custom, he now needed ritual cleansing in order to resume normal relations with his remaining wives. Part of the ritual involved the family of his dead wife providing a married woman for him to sleep with one time. As a Christian, he refused to do that. His own wives then retaliated by refusing to sleep with him or even to cook proper meals until he was "cleansed." What was he to do? Since his wives claimed to be Christians, it seemed the answer to this thorny question had to do with his own pastor who might counsel them about their Christian duty. This was one of the "ruins" Isaac had returned home to rebuild.

Even before he left his job on the chicken farm, Isaac used his leave days to evangelize, making the six-hundred mile round trip bus ride just to preach for a couple of days at his home. He began with his own extended family. He would later set up his new home in the kraal of his maternal uncle, James Siajeya, so this village became his starting point for ministry. His uncle was an *inyanga* (traditional healer), who called on spirits to diagnose and cure diseases. His kraal hardly seemed the best place to start a church, but nonetheless Isaac would bring his young family to live in a spiritualist village; this was also just the sort of ruins he sought to rebuild.

On one of his short visits back home, Isaac gathered the small group of seekers for worship under a *nyiyi* tree. Several of those who came out of curiosity manifested demonization and tried to run away from the preaching, but Isaac prayed for Jesus to take over; after that they calmed down and stayed to listen. His first convert was his cousin Mpendulo, a young man of boisterous temperament and outgoing spirit. Since Isaac only had a few days to stay during the two occasions he visited during his short times of leave from work on the chicken farm, he left his prized possession for Mpendulo and others to study: his only Tonga Bible. He told his new followers to begin reading Matthew 5, particularly the Beatitudes.

By the time Isaac had ministered thoroughly to this small group, they brought him two kilograms of "medicine" to destroy. "Medicine," also known as "*muthi*," which means "tree," comes from *inyangas*. They prescribe their own concoctions made from various natural products such as bark, roots, leaves, animal parts, and so on, as remedies for maladies ranging from intestinal illness to problems in marriage, from unemployment to barrenness, from worry to jealousy. While all Africans know about simple medicinal properties of plants, *muthi* from traditional healers comes with an extra spiritual dimension and is assumed to possess supernatural properties capable of curing whatever ails a person. *Inyangas* make all sorts of claims about having the ability to perform miracles because of their connections with the spirit world.

Church Planting

In downtown Bulawayo one day, I noticed a storefront that announced a traditional healer's services. Upon entering, I saw a very plain office space with a few differences. On the back wall was a huge python skin, and some traditional drums made up the rest of the office décor. Then out stepped the *inyanga* himself, dressed not in animal skins usually associated with traditional healers, but in a business suit, looking every ounce a professional medical man. He claimed to be one too, telling me he could cure AIDS.

This urban *inyanga* said that people from as far away as Europe had heard of his unique ability to cure the killer disease, and some Germans had even travelled to Zimbabwe to find out his secret. What was his secret, I asked, and how did he discover it? He replied that it was revealed to him by his ancestral spirit guide. The spirit told him which ingredients to use and how to administer the *muthi* to the terminally ill person. The source of the *inyanga*'s power comes from his or her spirit guide. All of his or her *muthi* is spirit-derived.

About the time that Isaac was ready to move to Magobbo to nurture his new converts into a church, he invited us to go and see what was already happening. A good-sized group of us undertook the long road trip, arriving at Isaac's village after dark on a pitch-black night. As usual, the Tongas gathered round us, talking, laughing, and greeting old friends and newcomers; after all, they had heard us coming a long way off. A strange sound that I could not identify that night mingled with the gabbling conversations: a sound of bubbles coming up through water. Only in the light of day next morning did I see that it came from homemade gourd pipes that some of the women were smoking.

These gourd pipes, popular among older Tonga women, were filled with water. On top of the gourd a hole was drilled where a sort of funnel was attached. The funnel was loaded with tobacco or marijuana, which was covered with a burning coal, with a cap on top of that. The women then drew the smoke from the burning substance down through the water into their mouths via the long stem of the gourd. It appeared that these large pipes were characteristic of Tonga women, along with having their two upper front teeth knocked out. At first I wondered if the teeth were removed in order to better insert the gourd stem into their mouths, but I was assured that that was not the case; no, the teeth were removed for beautification purposes. An additional beauty aid was often a stick through the nose between the nostrils. We were certainly in a different culture that even the Ndebele people with us found exotic.

49

Who Needs a Missionary?

Marijuana, called *imbanje* in Zimbabwe, is ubiquitous in Africa, freely grown and smoked, but often outlawed by governments. In the case of the Tongas, the Zimbabwean government made an exception. The Tonga homeland is the only part of Zimbabwe where smoking *imbanje* is legal; it appears the government knew it could not eradicate this habit in the Zambezi valley. Although the Tonga attachment to the weed is endemic, they are still not permitted to sell or transport it elsewhere.

The other more startling revelation that daylight brought to our newly arrived group was the fact that we had pitched our tents next to a new church building. Isaac had already organized the construction of a simple building even before he had actually moved back home. It was made from local materials such as the Tongas use for their own houses: poles and mud for the walls and thatched roof. Because of the hot climate year round, the walls only went about chest high to allow breezes to blow through. Benches were rough and simple: logs placed on forks of tree limbs that were driven into the mud and dung floor. Cow dung is mixed with mud to make a cement-like finish when it dries on the floor. There were doorways at the front and back but no doors, so the building was open at all times, allowing the occasional chicken to begin nesting inside. The podium was also made of poles and mud, with a crocheted cloth covering the top. Outside the building, hanging from a tree, was a long piece of metal that could be hit to announce the commencement of worship services, a form of church bell.

Isaac (on left) with his youth group outside the church he built.

Isaac soon introduced us to twenty-nine converts awaiting baptism. But what kind of converts could a first-grade dropout who was also a part-time evangelist produce? Ever skeptical, we missionaries wondered how well-taught these Tongas were. After all, Isaac had only had some vacation days to preach and teach, and we weren't sure that he himself had sufficient training. So we agreed with Isaac to interview all twenty-nine to see if they were really ready for baptism.

Since the majority of our entourage from Bulawayo did not speak Tonga, except for my colleague Allen Avery, who had spent ten years living in a Tonga village in Zambia, we had to rely on interpreters for the interviews. We divided up into several teams who conducted interviews so that each team ended up interviewing four or five candidates for baptism. The key questions we wanted to ask were: What were the Tongas repenting of that made them want to be baptized into Christ. What would change in their lives as a result of becoming followers of Jesus?

The answer given by a woman whom my team interviewed that day remains indelibly etched in my memory. As I asked what she was repenting of, the answer came back through the interpreter that she was repenting of using brown sugar in some way. Puzzled, I asked for clarification. She explained that as the wife of a man in a polygamous society, she desired to be his only wife. She had gone to a local *inyanga* to get some *muthi* that would make her husband have eyes for her alone. The problem was how to administer the *muthi*. That was where the brown sugar came in: the *muthi* could be mixed in with brown sugar and remain unnoticed. Her husband would then spoon the brown sugar into his morning cup of tea and imbibe the concoction unknowingly.

Concluding that this woman now understood that becoming a Christian meant a rejection of deceitful practices in her marriage and of using supernatural *muthi* from the *inyanga*, we gladly accepted her as a candidate for baptism. In fact, all our teams unanimously approved all twenty-nine interviewees as genuine converts. We had the distinct privilege of witnessing Isaac baptize all twenty-nine in a murky pond. It was a scene of great jubilation that remains one of the highlights of all my years of ministry in Zimbabwe.

Who Needs a Missionary?

Isaac baptizes one of twenty-nine new converts to start a church.

In case you are wondering about our cumbersome rite of interviewing candidates for baptism, let me give some background of our experiences with this important ordinance. Early on in our ministry at the Two Stamp Church, a man came asking for baptism. He was persistent in demanding with some urgency that he was ready and eager to become a Christian. Since we came from a tradition that saw no need to delay baptism once a person repented of sins and professed faith in Jesus as Savior, we complied and baptized the man. But as soon as we did, the man disappeared and we never saw him again. After some inquiry we concluded that the man, known to some of our Two Stamp members, regarded baptism as a magical act that would function much like an *inyanga*'s fetish to protect him from evil spirits.

Such experiences caused us to investigate more thoroughly whether a candidate for baptism was ready to take Jesus as Lord and not only as Savior. Spiritualists are experts at manipulating spirits, including Jesus, for their own perceived advantage. They need to know that God and Jesus will never be their servants; on the contrary, we become God's servants when we are born again. Far too many spiritualists never realize this and continue to seek assistance from *inyangas* in order to get spirits to do their bidding, even after baptism. Such syncretism has weakened Christianity wherever spiritualists live.

The flip side of this observation is that it is relatively easy to get spiritualists to be baptized, but not so easy for them to become true disciples of Jesus. Spiritualists seek spiritual inoculations against evil spirits, and the Christian ritual of baptism seems to promise the acquisition of Jesus as a powerful protector. Missionaries and churches that specialize in mass baptisms get to report startling numbers of converts. Even the African Initiated Churches have regular baptismal services, encouraging converts to be baptized over and over, so the "one baptism" of Ephesians 4:5 becomes multiple baptisms. The simple reason is that people from a spiritualist background tend to view baptism as a magical rite unless taught otherwise.

Because of this, we began to take more time counseling and teaching spiritualists before baptism. Allen Avery developed a short manual of questions we could ask a spiritualist in order to "clean house" when the person wished to repent and become a follower of Jesus. The house cleaning refers to Jesus' statement in Matthew 12:43–45 that an expelled evil spirit will roam around seeking a new place to inhabit. Finally it decides to return to where it was expelled to see if it can reenter. If it finds the house freshly swept and tidy, but still unoccupied, it not only reenters but also finds seven other spirits of an even more unsavory type to occupy and make the person's life more miserable than before.

The application of Jesus' teaching was originally aimed at the wicked generation of Jews, led by Pharisees, who continually attributed Jesus' ministry to the devil (Matt 12:24). Nevertheless, Jesus spent a lot of time trying to correct and reach the Pharisees, whom he saw as whitewashed tombs (Matt 23:27), appearing clean and orderly, but soon to be occupied by evil spirits if they did not submit to his lordship.

Likewise, spiritualists need a deep repentance and catharsis—to rid themselves of subjection to evil spirits and then to drink deeply of the Holy Spirit—to be able to reject any future inhabitation of other spirits. That takes some time; careful counseling and teaching is in order before and after baptism. After all, the goal is not just baptism, but the formation of disciples of Jesus. We concluded that Isaac had done a good job of preparing his converts for baptism, so there was no further need to delay.

All the activity in Magobbo that day did not go unnoticed by the neighbors. In a rural area the neighbors are not just next door but could live some miles away. Word travels quickly that a church meeting is taking place where there has not been a church, and those who consider themselves religious come over to check it out. Some Zionists from Kalonga came around that evening, dressed in their white labcoats decorated with green crosses.

Who Needs a Missionary?

They assumed this new church might be like theirs, so they came ready to participate in the worship services.

You might recall that Zionists are prevalent in southern Africa as examples of African Initiated Churches (AICs). The original Zionists formed by breaking away from more orthodox churches planted by white missionaries, and in reaction to white dominance in those churches. As a result, they are led entirely by Africans and their theology and practices often differ from those churches established by missionaries. On this occasion we were sitting in Isaac's newly constructed church building conducting a service when the sound of approaching drums could be heard. Soon they entered the building and joined in the worship.

The leader was decked out in a green cape with white embroidery and a matching head band, and was holding a shepherd's staff in his hand. He sat quietly during the meeting, but his followers were anything but quiet. Because of their exuberance it was often hard to tell whose meeting it was, theirs or ours. Yet in hopes of being able to win them over, and because in Africa blunt confrontation is unacceptable, we did our best to carry on the meeting to its conclusion without rebuking them.

When our service concluded, they began their own service. Since they had already heard preaching they went on to their next stage of worship: dancing. They went round and round in a circle beating drums and singing choruses with some Christian content. At times the dancers would begin foot-stomping and jumping up and down with great vertical leaps. Since it was the dry season the ground was dusty, so foot-stomping created billowing clouds of white dust that enveloped the dancers and everyone around them. Disregarding this inconvenience, the young dancers not only tolerated the choking dust, but actually lowered their heads into it, so that soon the dust clung to their heads, creating a sort of halo effect on their black hair. It was a riveting scene but not one we had come prepared for.

Zionists are known for all night *pungwes*, or dancing services. This has unfortunately led to some promiscuity among their youth and even older members, as they prefer nighttime in the bush for these activities. Now they were right on our doorstep, so to speak, as our tent was adjacent to the church building and they were dancing outside the church for the duration. We attempted to sleep and eventually were able to, as we were all exhausted from travel and a full day's activities with the new converts. Nevertheless, the Zionists kept waking us up from time to time. Allen Avery had a history of strange behavior when asleep, sometimes sleep-walking and sometimes

Church Planting

talking in his sleep. This night was no exception because of the many interruptions to sound sleep.

A one point Allen sat up and spoke to some Africans in our tent: "Those singers don't have a license to be making this noise at this time of night. Go and tell them they don't have a license and they must stop!" Not realizing Allen was actually asleep, they dutifully went and delivered the message, but it fell on deaf ears. Later, he sat up again and said, "I thought I had my gun under my pillow. It's not here and I need it. Go and look for my gun in the car!" Again an African went out to search the car for a gun, but with no success. That was probably a good thing, because we had no clue what a sleeping man might do with a loaded gun!

This particular trip was made in July 1987, when Isaac was still employed on the Wolhuters' chicken farm. He had not even moved back to Magobbo yet. Even then the challenges and obstacles in the way of planting a church were quite obvious to all of us. Nevertheless, Isaac proceeded undaunted to quit his job and move his family north into the Zambezi valley in the month of November that year. I noted in a newsletter that he soon baptized another fourteen people (without our interviewing any of them). With more candidates preparing for baptism, his membership grew to nearly fifty new converts. In addition he aimed to plant a second church during the dry season of 1988, after he finished harvesting his first crops as a self-supporting farmer.

Isaac and Margaret with their two older sons soon after returning home.

Who Needs a Missionary?

For that new church he approached Chief Sinampande both to witness to him personally about Jesus and also to seek approval to launch a new church in his domain. The chief pointed him to the Sinampande Primary School for Sunday meetings. Isaac began in Sinampande's area as he had done in Magobbo, visiting in homes and preaching each evening, until he had enough people interested in forming a church.

Isaac invited Allen Avery to return with a team to help out at Sinampande. Among those who went with Allen were George Mpofu, Obert Ncube, Fibion Nyevhe, Johnson Maphosa, and Mukesh Naik. Most of these were young men, some still teenagers, full of enthusiasm and faith. They were also from various backgrounds: George and Johnson were Ndebeles, Fibion was Shona, Obert was one of the squatters from Two Stamp, and Mukesh was from an Indian family. The multicultural team visibly demonstrated the diversity of the body of Christ.

Obert was one of the first people we baptized in Zimbabwe. After attending our first church at Two Stamp for some months, Obert and other youngsters asked to be baptized. At the time he was about to finish primary school and was in his early teens. Mari-Etta and I organized a five-week pre-baptismal course for them to go through in preparation, complete with illustrations that professional teachers like Mari-Etta are skilled at producing. The course was attended by up to twenty youths, but in the end only ten were actually baptized in early 1982. We trekked down to the Umguza River, which meanders around the city of Bulawayo, right past the squatter camp. It has pools of water until the dry season in mid-year evaporates them. Bernard Madlopha and I were the baptizers, and neither of us had performed many baptisms, so it was almost as exciting for us as it was for the youths, who were exuberant.

After the government burned down Two Stamp in 1983, as it was an illegal squatter camp, we tried to keep up with Obert and his family, but eventually lost track of him. Years later, when he was almost an adult, we encountered him again. We discovered he had become a free-lance evangelist in Chief Sigola's area, not far from the old squatter camp. He took biblical examples seriously, going out without purse or extra gear, seeking out a person of peace to reside with (Matt 10:10-11). He would preach for repentance and acceptance of Christ and live on whatever food his host provided. We persuaded him that his talents could be used in a team with us; he readily rejoined our ministry and was never shy of tackling the most formidable assignments for God.

Church Planting

Planting a church at Sinampande turned out to be just such a formidable task, primarily because the familiar issue of demonization appeared once again. With the visitors' team present at the evening service in the primary school, one woman began to manifest a demon during the prayer time for the sick. People told Isaac that this woman had such a strong demon that it could not be conquered; in fact, it had defeated every church so far. Isaac's response was, "This demon is now meeting Jesus, not a church!" The woman collapsed on the floor and the whole team rushed over to rebuke the demon. In their haste, each one was doing and saying something different. One was yelling for the demon to come out, another was telling the demon to state its name, another asking where it had come from, and yet another was pressing a Bible against the woman. Isaac held back, viewing the chaotic scene and wishing for more order and unity of approach.

These unruly scenes usually came at two times: during baptism and public prayers for the sick or for those wishing to become Christians. The disruption is often more widespread and intense when a new ministry is just starting. Sinampande certainly provided a vivid example of this scenario. Now, as another lady came to maintain the modesty of the demonized woman by making sure that her dress covered her legs, she too fell over demonized. The team from Bulawayo rushed over to her, leaving the first woman unattended. Isaac took advantage of the situation to calmly drive out the first woman's demon. Then he called for the group to settle down to confront the demonic activity in a more orderly fashion.

Meanwhile other people in the gathering were collapsing. Isaac called for the team to split up into small groups who could concentrate on one person at a time, praying for and receiving deliverance. By using "Jesus and order" (in Isaac's words), the group not only restored calm, but delivered numerous people from demonization to become followers of Christ. To the amazement of the local community, the nightly meetings led to the formation of a new church.

Part of the amazement had to do with the type of demon that caused the disruption of the service: the *ngozi* spirit. While the Ndebele and Shona peoples of Zimbabwe speak of *ngozi* as an avenging spirit, the Tongas use the term to refer to an ancestral spirit who makes the person it possesses act like an animal. In either case it is recognized to be a difficult spirit to exorcise. Isaac said that the characteristic of the *ngozi* spirit in his home area is that it makes the person drink goat's blood, and this was the spirit of the first woman to manifest demonization at Sinampande. Now, Isaac noted, "she has drunk the blood of Jesus and she is okay."

Who Needs a Missionary?

An unexpected result of this church plant was that a neighboring Methodist Church dwindled to a single member who remained with Pastor Muzamba. This concerned Isaac, who had not intended to build a church at the expense of other churches, but to win those who had never believed in Jesus. He decided to give over all his new converts to Pastor Muzamba and to relocate a couple of kilometers away at a place called Chilamba where he started another church that still exists under the leadership of Edward Mweembe and Joseph Munsaka. In this way, Isaac gained the trust and respect of older churches for refusing to poach members or infringe on their territory. In return, his influence caused them to be more evangelical, intent on helping spiritualists reorient to true Christianity.

Mark and I camped out in this tent in Isaac's village.

By the time Mark Elefritz and I visited Isaac at Magobbo in 1989, he had both churches established. We began a short intense period of daily evangelism with Isaac and his converts in the area between Magobbo and Chilamba. We pitched our two-man tent in Isaac's village, actually that of his Uncle James Siajeya, the *inyanga*—although we weren't aware of that at the time. I recall finding a cow horn that was being used as a container for *muthi*; when I asked what was in the horn, the response was snake bite antivenin, primarily for rubbing on dogs that got snake bites. Now I wonder if there was more to that *muthi* than what I was told.

Church Planting

This is rough country that we were in. We had walked five miles off the nearest road, built by Rhodesian troops during the civil war that led to Zimbabwe's independence. The gravel road had fallen into disrepair, becoming corrugated and pocked with potholes during the rainy seasons, with little maintenance now being done. Our walk from the main road down tracks used by animal-drawn carts took us away from Lake Kariba toward a range of hills that stood guard over Isaac's village. Over the hills lay Chizarira National Park, full of wild animals that ventured onto Tonga land, especially during harvest time. The Tongas were familiar with all the game animals from the smallest duiker to the mighty elephant, from the rock rabbit to the lion, as all of them sometimes frequented their living space. Like most Africans, they love game meat, but most don't own firearms, so they set illegal snares. At the same time, elephants and lions have the advantage when it comes to raiding.

Isaac and I, with a Tonga boy sitting on an elephant skull.

The main water source for the villagers is a river running down from the hills, through which it has carved a notch over the millennia. As with other Zimbabwean rivers, with the exception of the mighty Zambezi, this one dries up in mid-year after the rains end and it stays dry until the return of the rainy season at the year's end. My wife, Mari-Etta, familiar with American rivers of the Pacific Northwest where her family used to spend summer vacations, would insist that dry rivers are not rivers at all. I would reply that we used to ask this riddle growing up in Zimbabwe: "What do you do when you fall into a Zimbabwean river?" The answer: "Get up and dust yourself off."

But even a dry river is a water source, as villagers dig in the sand to find the water percolating just a few feet under the riverbed. Elephants also know how to find it this way, following the river down through the hills, with drinking water always available by digging. But that source of water can become scarce too, so the government has dug a few boreholes along the river bank to get to deeper pockets of water. The borehole near Isaac's village produces water so rich with salts that it is hard to drink.

We preferred that the water be used for making tea, as that way it was not only boiled for purification, but also made palatable. Tea was probably the British government's best gift to places like Zimbabwe, as it has become the national breakfast drink of choice in every location, rural and urban. Few would want to start the day without a steaming cup of tea to wash down some slices of bread, until the collapse of the Zimbabwean economy crushed even that simple pleasure for many. In 1989, however, we had brought fresh bread from town bakeries. When that supply ran out, Isaac's wife, Margaret, fried *amaqebelengwana*, lumps of self-rising flour mixed with sugar and dropped in hot oil to make a facsimile of a doughnut.

Other than the boreholes, there is no visible evidence of government services where Isaac lives. His area is so remote that villagers need not ask permission to build kraals in new locations from anyone, even their chief. The raw bush country is wide open for them to settle, clear, build, and cultivate as they see fit. Shortage of water is the only constraint.

After our morning bath from a bucket followed by breakfast, we would set out towards Chilamba, angling back toward the main road without reaching it, evangelizing kraals along the way. That is how we met perhaps the oldest African I have ever known, named Chilawela. He was usually sitting outside his hut as we walked by, too old to work, but still enjoying the morning air and visitors. He said he remembered hearing about Ndebele warriors passing near the area with their last king, Lobhengula. This refers to the demise of the Ndebele kingdom in 1893 when the British attacked and destroyed their capital near Bulawayo. Lobhengula fled northwest with his most trusted *impis* guarding him, only to disappear from history, never to be found again. Tongas deeply feared the Ndebele for the raids they conducted to steal cattle and women, so the final intrusion of Lobhengula's forces must have made quite an impact on Chilawela's young life. That would have made the old man somewhere in his nineties at least.

The other remarkable thing about Chilawela is that when he heard the gospel message of salvation in Jesus, he wanted to become a Christian! Rarely will adult men respond positively to the gospel, and older people are usually set in their ways, so for such an old man to declare for Jesus when his family were all non-Christians is truly remarkable. After Mark and I left the area, Isaac organized Chilawela's baptism. Since the old man was not able to walk to the nearest pond, Isaac brought his bicycle over, sat him on the saddle, and wheeled him to the water for baptism. Isaac had the privilege of both baptizing and later burying Chilawela. When I visited the area in 2010, I was able to meet Chilawela's son, Moses, now also a Christian. But the story of how his family became Christians must wait until a later chapter.

The Why and How of Church Planting

With today's diverse mission theories we need to begin with the question: Why focus on evangelism and church planting? In Isaac's case, he established a church first, even before he moved his family to Binga District. Many today question that strategy, given that the Tongas are a forgotten people in a neglected region, with overwhelming physical needs. So why start with spiritual needs? The answer, pure and simple, is that spiritual needs run even deeper than physical needs and sometimes cause them.

In the pendulum swing of American mission emphasis, we have gone back and forth on this issue for a century now. At the moment, our emphasis has swung to meeting physical needs by all means.[1] Since we have the material resources, we should use them to alleviate poverty and the issues that go with it. By doing that, we earn the right to deal also with spiritual problems. There is some truth to this emphasis, but in Isaac's case there is a difference: he is an insider who knows his culture thoroughly and he sees the central need as making Jesus known and challenging people to follow him. Does he then neglect physical needs? In a later chapter we will see the answer to that is no, but Isaac did not see it as the place to start.

If we take a look at Scripture, we soon see some support for Isaac's stance. Take for instance the first action of the Holy Spirit after the ascension of Jesus into heaven. On the Day of Pentecost, the Spirit descended on the waiting disciples in Jerusalem enabling them to proclaim the "wonders of God" in multiple languages at once (Acts 2:4–11). Peter's sermon

1. Rowell, *To Give or Not To Give?*, 141-5.

explained how the miracle of tongues happened and what the Spirit meant by sending it (Acts 2:16–21). He showed emphatically from the Old Testament how the resurrected Jesus is the promised Messiah, whom his audience had recently crucified (Acts 2:29–36). His words cut the people to their hearts and resulted in the formation of the first church that same day (Acts 2:41). Immediately afterwards, the newly organized church began to meet both spiritual and physical needs, which were many (Acts 2:42–45).

The rest of the Book of Acts shows that evangelists and apostles began to preach and plant churches everywhere they could, but always with the leading and prompting of the Holy Spirit. Indeed, the book could just as easily be called "Acts of the Holy Spirit" as Acts of the Apostles. For example, when Christians seemed to be content with the healthy growth of the original church in Jerusalem, the Holy Spirit used persecution to drive evangelists out into the surrounding countryside of Judea and Samaria (Acts 8:1–4). In this way, churches were planted in those locations too. When the apostles seemed content to limit evangelism to Jews and Samaritans, the Holy Spirit intervened again to compel Peter to preach to a Roman centurion, Cornelius (Acts 10:9–20). This Gentile was baptized along with his family and friends in the Spirit, just as the apostles were on the Day of Pentecost (Acts 10:44–46). When Antioch became the first major center for Gentile converts, the Holy Spirit selected the first cross-cultural mission team that we know about, Saul of Tarsus and Barnabas (Acts 13:1–2). This team proceeded to plant churches in the eastern part of the Roman Empire and Saul, better known as Paul, went on to plant churches right into what is now known as Europe. All this activity was conducted by the Holy Spirit, showing emphatically that the Great Commission involved church planting.

Jesus issued the Great Commission five times in various locations, using different words (Matt 28:19–20; Mark 16:15–16; Luke 24:47; John 20:21; Acts 1:8). The most commonly used version is Matthew's, where Jesus explicitly commands his followers to make more disciples by going out to all nations, baptizing and teaching them. This strongly implies the necessity of planting churches. Four of the five versions of the Great Commission emphasize preaching, witnessing, and teaching. The other one, John 20:21, is taken by some today to be more holistic and therefore more relevant to our time.[2] This is because Jesus says in this verse that our mission is modeled on his.

---

2. Stott, *Christian Mission in the Modern World*, 23.

John Stott, an influential spokesman for evangelicalism, believes that the incarnational model of mission, based on John 20:21, places social and spiritual needs on the same plane; he states, "Social action is a partner of evangelism. . . . Neither is a means to the other, or even a manifestation of the other. For each is an end in itself."[3] Stott's approach links the Great Commission to the Great Commandment, the injunction to love God and love our neighbor (Matt 22:37–9). While there is merit in this linkage, there can easily be misunderstanding too. Let's take a look at how Jesus combined evangelism with social action.

Jesus was clearly concerned about social issues but not necessarily in the same way we tend to be. Western people tend to approach social and physical problems through the application of superior human ability; we usually try to tackle these problems by political action, ingenuity, or financial strength. Jesus operated out of none of these paradigms that we consider essential to "making a difference." He stripped himself of visible resources before beginning ministry. This made it appear that he had little to offer those in need, while in actuality he had what they most needed: himself. We too have Jesus to offer to those in any kind of need, but we often fixate on the material resources we have first.

For example, consider the time when Jesus fed five thousand men, plus women and children, in a remote location near the Sea of Galilee (John 6:10–13). This was an act of sheer compassion because the crowds had followed him into a region with no stores and they were hungry. He and his disciples had few resources with which to feed the people, so it had to be done by a miracle. The people recognized the greatness of the miracle and wished to crown Jesus as their king, but he slipped away from them up a mountain alone (John 6:15). He rejected their adulation because he sensed that their appreciation for the free meal skewed their understanding of who he was and how he operated.

Later, when the crowds caught up to Jesus back in Capernaum, he made it clear why he withdrew from them just after feeding them: "I tell you the truth, you are looking for me, not because you saw miraculous signs but because you ate the loaves and had your fill. Do not work for food that spoils, but for food that endures to eternal life, which the Son of Man will give you" (John 6:26–27). Then he offered himself to them as the bread of life that would let them "never go hungry" (John 6:35). When he told

---

3. Ibid., 27.

them to eat of himself, many refused to listen further and left in disgust (John 6:52, 66).

In this case, it was not so much Jesus himself the crowds wanted as it was the food he gave them. That is often how it is with trying to meet physical needs. Those with plenty of resources may be able to provide lots of material assistance and receive the adulation of the recipients of their largesse, but that may also create expectations for continuous help with those needs. Physical needs tend to abound more than solutions. As Jesus pointed out, those who ate the one meal he gave them soon got hungry again. Even manna was inferior to what Jesus offered: "Your forefathers ate manna and died, but he who feeds on this bread [himself] will live forever" (John 6:58). The contrast he draws is between physical food—that may even be provided repeatedly, as manna was for forty years—and eternal food which outlives this life. Eternity cannot ever really compare to anything temporary.

John uses the word "sign" to denote this and other key miracles in his gospel. "Sign" indicates that the miracle pointed to a greater truth than just the obvious amazement that so easily captured people's imagination. In every case, Jesus' signs pointed to himself. Jesus is the ultimate need that all people have, whether they know it or not. That is why church planting is essential in obeying the Great Commission, as it puts the lordship of Jesus front and center over all other gods.

Take another example from the Gospel of Luke. Along the border between Samaria and Galilee, Jesus encountered ten lepers, who stood at a distance as outcastes and yelled for mercy from the miracle-worker (Luke 17:11–13). Again Jesus responded out of pure compassion and told them all to present themselves to the priests for the ritual that would restore them to regular society; as they went on their way they were all healed (Luke 17:14). One of them, a Samaritan, returned to thank Jesus and to praise God for his healing. Jesus responded, "Were not all ten cleansed? Where are the other nine?" (Luke 17:17). As in the case of the feeding of the five thousand, the physical help Jesus gave did not automatically cause repentance or salvation. He significantly told the Samaritan, "Rise and go; your faith has made you well" (Luke 17:19), implying that the Samaritan had received more than physical healing.

This reminds me of an outstanding evangelist I sometimes worked with named Lovemore Lunga. Lovemore was something of a free-lance evangelist, preferring to work alone to the beat of his own drum. Nevertheless, he agreed to work with us for a while. Of all the people I knew in Zimbabwe who preached or evangelized, Lovemore seemed to have the most obvious gift of healing. First Corinthians 12:9 refers to the gift of healing given to some by the Holy Spirit to use in ministry, and we noticed that Lovemore could pray for people and see them healed quite often. In fact, he developed a reputation for this gift among groups that knew him.

On one occasion I accompanied him to a place where we were planting a new church near the Mbembesi River on the Victoria Falls road. Lovemore also happened to have married a woman from this village, so he was well known in the immediate area. Once we arrived, people began to show up and ask him to pray for their healing. Among Zimbabweans, healing by prayer is often sought, partly because of wide-spread belief in supernatural cures effected by *inyangas,* and also because of lack of Western medical facilities. Many churches, especially African Initiated Churches, specialize in healing services. Lovemore, on the other hand, was a one-man show with a growing reputation.

So I sat in a small hut belonging to Lovemore's in-laws to watch how he operated. Outside, the queue of people coming for prayers grew longer. Lovemore admitted the patients one at a time into the hut and would counsel and pray for them as I merely observed. I wanted to learn about his gift and see how contextualized healing is done by an experienced evangelist. With the door closed and only the three of us in the room, Lovemore would ask where the pain was located. Then he would place one hand on the area of pain, the other hand on the head of the kneeling person, and pray a brief but forceful prayer. He would then lean down to ask about the pain again. Surprisingly to me, the person would sometimes say the pain had relocated elsewhere, perhaps from one side of the abdomen to the other. Lovemore then prayed a second time and again inquired about the pain. After the second prayer most people stated that the pain had gone and left rejoicing in the cure.

Lovemore's method was very direct, brief, and forceful. He would not tolerate the presence of fetishes on people he was about to pray for. I remember one large church service when Lovemore was about to pray for a kneeling man who sported a Saint Christopher's medal as a necklace. The man was not a church member and probably believed the medal gave him luck. Saint Christopher is a patron of travelers, and his medallions often adorn vehicles like taxis and long-distance trucks. But Lovemore simply said, "You won't need this anymore," and yanked the medal off the man's neck, breaking the chain. I still remember seeing the shock on the man's face at this abrupt seizure of his trusted fetish.

Who Needs a Missionary?

On another occasion, Lovemore showed his ability to compete with *inyangas* by "smelling out" fetishes hidden in boxes. We were in the back room of the church building at Emakhandeni Community Church in Bulawayo when Lovemore suddenly claimed that some of the boxes stored there contained fetishes dedicated to *amadlozi* (ancestral spirits). Elliot Donga, pastor of the church, was quite perturbed to hear this accusation. Nevertheless, he ordered that the boxes be opened and checked. Sure enough, the contents of the boxes included items dedicated to *amadlozi*, specifically *amahlwayi*, the leggings containing seed pods that rattle when the person wearing them dances for the spirits. The items belonged to German Dube's brother who had recently died; his property was being temporarily stored in the church building until his relatives could reclaim it. But how did Lovemore know the items were in the boxes? It seems he just had some uncanny ability to sense things supernaturally and I have no explanation beyond that.

Lovemore's story is more sensational than Isaac's, begging the question of why this book is not about him. The answer is that Isaac's ministry resulted in long-term transformation, while Lovemore's did not. After I worked with Lovemore for several years, it became clear that he actually had relatively few converts and had planted no churches that I knew of. His celebrity status also carried temptations to cash in on his skills, which he eventually did. His personal failings also contributed to the termination his marriage. Both Lovemore and Isaac were very independent in their work, but Lovemore was independent to the point of being difficult to work with. I don't know how Lovemore has ended up; as for Isaac, I have seen the fruit of his work preserved in churches that helped bring about a positive impact on the whole community.

Perhaps the problem we have with church planting in the West is that we are so disappointed with existing churches. Most of us have experienced sadness in relating to local churches, which all too often seem insular and self-absorbed, not impacting the surrounding community. But let us not confuse our limited experience with a clear biblical ecclesiology. A study of the New Testament reveals the close association between the church and the Trinity. Multiple images are given for the church: the family of God, the body of Christ, the bride of Christ, and the temple of the Holy Spirit.

Paul says that the church reveals the "manifold wisdom of God . . . to the rulers and authorities in the heavenly realms" (Eph 3:10). This wisdom is evident through the integration of Jews and Gentiles into the church, both sharing in the promise of God in Christ (Eph 3:6). Paul explains that Christ alone made it possible for Jews and Gentiles to belong together as "members of God's household" (Eph 2:19). God's family has room for all, with none who believe in Christ remaining foreigners or second-class citizens any longer. Galatians 3:28 states, "There is neither Jew nor Greek, slave nor free, male nor female, for you are all one in Christ Jesus." When I become a Christian, regardless of my background, I enter the same family that belonged to Abraham, Isaac, and Jacob, and I truly belong even though I was adopted. The Spirit tells me that I am God's child (Rom 8:16), and that makes all other Christians my brothers and sisters.

In addition to the image of the family of God, Paul also likens the church to the body of Christ, a unified organism with diverse parts. "We were all baptized by one Spirit into one body—whether Jews or Greeks, slave or free" (1 Cor 12:13). Being one body implies both that Christ is in charge and that we all have work to do under his direction. Colossians 1:18 says, "And he is the head of the body, the church . . . so that in everything he might have the supremacy." In directing the body, he assigns gifts to each part so that all have a role to play in the health and function of the body. Some have gifts of leadership or evangelism, pastoring or teaching, so that the church is built up in unity and maturity (Eph 4:11–13). But no Christian is simply along for the ride as a member of the body of Christ. The church is literally the hands and feet of Jesus on earth today.

Paul also calls the church the temple of the Holy Spirit. That makes it the only human organization that is also inhabited by the divine. The Holy Spirit makes the church a body of worshippers who strive to draw all others who are outside into the worship that rightfully belongs to God. When writing to the Corinthian church, Paul was deeply disappointed that they were dividing over which preacher to follow (1 Cor 1:12–13). That caused him to reflect on the nature of the church, and he told the Corinthians that they had crossed the line when they deliberately destroyed the unity of the temple of the Holy Spirit because of a popularity contest (1 Cor 3:16–17). The Holy Spirit makes the local church sacred as a place where worship of the true God takes place corporately.

Finally, the church is the bride of Christ. Paul likens the marriage bond between husband and wife to the relationship between Christ and the church (Eph 5:25). Jesus cares for and cleanses the church as a husband should care for and protect his wife. Unlike human marriage, Christ is linked eternally with his bride in Revelation 19:7. The wedding feast of the

Lamb and his bride is presented as a great celebration in heaven after Christ subdues his final enemies. Thus, whatever we may feel or experience about local churches we know of, it is good to remember that each church is part of the everlasting bride of Christ. Even when Paul was disappointed with a church, such as the one in Corinth, he still asserted that it was "sanctified in Christ Jesus and called to be holy" (1 Cor 1:2).

We need just as elevated a view of the church as Paul had. Perhaps we have settled for ideas of the church that fall short of biblical ecclesiology. Perhaps we have even decided the church is irrelevant to God's real plans. The Bible, however, does not agree. Rather, the church is to be the agent of God's kingdom on earth. In seeking a theology of social action, most scholars arrive at the concept of the kingdom of God, where God's will is done on earth as it is in heaven (Matt 6:10). Taking God's kingdom to be his rule over creation, the concept of the kingdom of God means that communities on earth start to live according to God's rule for all of creation. That encompasses any kind of social action necessary to bring the community into compliance with God's will.

This is precisely where many local churches fall short, in that they not only fail to impact the community towards God's will, but they also do not even obey God themselves. Each church should obviously be incorporated into God's kingdom, explicitly striving to follow God's will in every way. Then clear aspects of God's design, such as truth-telling, honest business dealings, love of neighbor, and evangelism will be practiced. Beyond these, churches will also show good stewardship of resources, support for strong families, healthy personal interaction, concern for the poor, and biblical leadership principles through service. But notice that all these emphases of God's kingdom are best done in the church, with the local church showing the non-Christian community what God's kingdom is like. That is precisely what happened in the churches Isaac planted, but we will save that for a later chapter, because it did not happen quickly. Churches had to be planted first in order for social action to take place within the body and then out in the community.

As far as the how of church planting, nothing can improve on the apostle Paul's methods. As shown in the Book of Acts, he always began by preaching at the Jewish synagogue if there was one in that location. He was usually rejected by the majority of Jews who were not convinced Jesus was Messiah. But those Jews whom he won, along with the God-fearing Gentiles who believed his message, formed a nucleus of potential leaders for churches. Paul also preached in marketplaces and homes in search of converts. These converts he formed into simple house churches with designated leaders whom he trained to function as a team.

From the start, Paul's churches were what we now call "Three-Self" churches: self-governing, self-supporting, and self-propagating.[4] All three, plus the "Fourth Self" proposed by Paul Hiebert, self-theologizing,[5] are important as a combination for healthy churches. The ability to make their own leadership decisions, to fund their own ministries, and to equip and send evangelists or missionaries, along with the capacity to interpret Scriptures for themselves, makes for powerfully functioning local churches that fulfill the purpose God has for them.

Summary

From the book of Acts, we see that planting a church was the first agenda of the Holy Spirit on the Day of Pentecost. We also see that Paul began to plant churches after his conversion, again following the Holy Spirit's lead. New Testament churches were beacons of light to their neighbors wherever they were planted. The more churches, the more light shed into the communities where they were located. Churches were the agents of God's kingdom, showing the life of the Spirit in a world in darkness. Because Christians espoused countercultural lifestyles, they were either loved or hated, but they consistently stood for biblical principles in a hostile world. Yet they continued to reach out to their non-Christian neighbors through acts of kindness and evangelism.

Isaac instinctively followed Paul's methods closely. He began by preaching to his neighbors and friends, meeting under trees, and conducting spiritual warfare to release people from the grip of evil spirits. He also welcomed assistance from other evangelical Christians from various backgrounds, who would be equivalent to the Jews and God-fearing Gentiles whom Paul encountered. Isaac always maintained good relations as far as he could with other evangelical churches, and this eventually gave him considerable influence in his home region.

For his own leaders, Isaac mostly relied on training them up himself, which is the soundest method. Since the training up of new leaders is essential to developing Four-Self churches, we will save this for Chapter 6.

4. Reese, *Roots and Remedies*, 154–63.
5. Hiebert, *Anthropological Insights*, 196.

Who Needs a Missionary?

For the long-term health of new churches, nothing can substitute for quality leaders who make godly decisions, give of time, talent, and money, take the gospel to unbelievers, and use the Bible wisely. In one sense making converts in a place like Africa is fairly easy, but developing outstanding leaders is much harder, yet equally essential. Isaac managed to do both, just as Paul did, but he also had to make a living to support his family.

4

Making a Living

It's all well and good to have a strong calling from God to go and do something, but practical considerations also come into focus very soon. After his long sojourn away from Magobbo, Isaac was bringing home a new Ndebele wife, Margaret, and a growing family. We already mentioned Nomsa, his firstborn girl, born the same year as our Ellen in 1980. Later came four sons: Lazarus, Moses, Benjamin, and Jewel, followed by a surprise final daughter, Lydia, in 2006. By the time Lydia was born, Isaac and Margaret already had grandchildren.

Isaac with Nomsa, Lazarus, and Moses in the late 1980s.

Who Needs a Missionary?

Of course, God's call and practical considerations are never really in opposition, unless we make them so. If we set them in competition, it's like saying that God doesn't know or care about our daily lives, or perhaps he overlooked reality. Hardly possible for the God who created reality! It's much more credible to think that we don't have enough faith in God to supply our needs.

Isaac's faith was not in short supply, as he willingly and deliberately left a paying job with employers who were every bit as devoted to him as he was to them. Even to this day, one of his first questions to me when we meet is whether I have any news from the Wolhuters. Usually I don't, because they left Zimbabwe for Australia long ago, making it difficult to keep in touch. During the time when they operated the chicken farm, the Wolhuters represented stability and safety for Isaac's family.

God's call was so strong on Isaac, however, that he forsook safety for uncertainty. He didn't ask for advice or seek support, because he was so sure he was doing the right thing. Of course, there were no guarantees that his family would be okay. The ancient African safety net was there, to be sure; the extended family would always take them in and help to feed them. That's why Isaac lived with his maternal uncle first. But he never intended to take advantage of his uncle, so he timed his arrival home with the start of the growing season, when he could easily get a field and begin planting. He intended to be a farmer just as his ancestors had been for centuries before him.

Farmers know that their business is one of the most unpredictable. For the Tongas, success in farming depends on numerous factors far beyond their control: weather, wild animals, birds, good health, and witchcraft. That is why most African farmers grow just enough to live on, practicing subsistence farming. Or, in some cases, they grow almost too little to live on, in order to keep witchcraft at bay.

A friend of ours, Jim Harries, left his home country of England to go to Zambia as an agricultural missionary. He quickly spotted a way that he could help Zambian farmers avoid what they called the "hungry months." That was the gap between the time when last year's harvest ran out and this year's harvest ripened. Jim noted that all the farmers in that part of Zambia expected to go without adequate food for their families for a couple of months each year. He also noted that by simply extending their fields by a few acres, they could avoid this shortfall.

Making a Living

When he approached one farmer with this simple suggestion, he was surprised by the response: "If I grow extra food, I will have to supply the other villagers with food for the hungry months." Jim asked, "Why would you have to give your supply of food away?" The response was: "If I should produce extra food, while others do not, I become the target of witchcraft. To avoid witchcraft, I must give away my excess food. So I am not going to enlarge my field."

At that point, Jim realized that food shortages in Zambia and elsewhere in Africa often have nothing to do with sound agricultural techniques, but with spiritualism. From that time on, he quit being an agricultural specialist and went into what he calls "Vulnerable Missions."[1] He decided to drop the notion of bringing outside resources to rural Africans; he simply lived in a village in Kenya in order to learn the rural African mindset in local language categories so he could minister more effectively.

While Isaac immediately jumped into subsistence farming, he also tried his hand at the closest cash-producing occupation for Tongas: net fishing in the rivers that run into Lake Kariba. He bought a fishnet and went to Mujele fishing camp down the road from his home.

It was really the formation of Lake Kariba in the late 1950s that introduced the Tongas to globalization. The Rhodesian government of that time alerted the Tongas that many of their villages near the Zambezi River would be flooded by the construction of a giant dam at Kariba. Lake Kariba was the world's largest man-made lake at that time, and thousands of Tonga villages were inundated by the rising water, necessitating mass movement away from the river.

Not only people but wild animals were put in danger. My first memory of the Zambezi was in late 1959, when my brother John and I spent our school holidays at a Game Department camp on the shores of Lake Kariba almost in the shadow of the dam wall. My father was working there with Operation Noah, an effort to rescue the large numbers of wild animals that were endangered by the rising waters. All varieties of wildlife moved to high ground that soon became islands, some of which were then submerged in the vast lake.

Operation Noah aimed to capture and move these animals to safer ground. Some were rescued from the water itself, as they tried to swim to dry ground. This effort caught the world's attention even more than the plight of the Tongas, bringing an international spotlight to a forgotten

---

1. Harries, *Vulnerable Missions*.

valley. Not since David Livingstone explored the Zambezi River valley in the mid-nineteenth century had the international community paid so much attention to the Tonga homeland.

Italians built the dam and lived so long at Kariba town that there is a captivating circular Catholic cathedral there. Kariba became and remained a cosmopolitan little town built on the hills above the dam, a vacation destination for many tourists in the good old days. In the early 1980s our family journeyed from one end of Lake Kariba to the other by ferry, with our vehicle onboard, so we could attend a missionary conference at the Most High Hotel in Kariba town. To give you an idea of the lake's size, that ferry ride took twenty-four hours.

Kapenta fish were introduced to the lake as a source of commercial fishing. Soon you could see dozens of fishing boats with their circular nets resembling large satellite dishes. They fish at night for these sardines, using bright lights to attract the shoals of fish. The tiny kapenta are salted, dried, and packaged in plastic bags for mass consumption. They have become a staple source of cheap protein for Zimbabwean and Zambian families. I remember one time when a young man took his turn cooking for our evangelistic group. He salted the kapenta, which were already very salty, so it tasted as if we were eating pure salt with the *isitshwala*. I am still not fond of kapenta, but many people are.

And other fish are fond of eating kapenta, making Lake Kariba a fisherman's paradise. Because the Tongas had fished the Zambezi for centuries, they were given the right to continue doing that, but now they had to fish the tributaries of the inland sea. They would spread out their nets across the mouths of streams entering the lake, and then salt and dry the many varieties of fish they caught, such as bream, chessa, and tiger fish. These were then bundled in wooden frames tied with bark string and placed on long-distance buses for sale in urban areas hundreds of miles away. That is the business Isaac tried out first.

Mujele fishing camp is one of the main places Tongas attempt to make a living from fishing. Such places attract hustlers and profiteers trying to take advantage of village folks. Prostitution is rife and so is the spread of HIV. The seamier side of globalization is the use and abuse of humans, where accountability doesn't exist in relationships. Mujele was not an ideal place for a man called to preach the gospel to make a decent living.

As it turned out, after one week of fishing, Isaac had caught nothing. Furthermore, Bible verses kept coming to mind that he was supposed to be rebuilding the broken walls of Tonga life, as Nehemiah had done for Jerusalem, and he was supposed to be a fisher of men instead of fish. So he abruptly turned his net over to a relative and returned to Magobbo, having lost money in his first attempt at commercial activity.

Next he tried cotton farming. This is where we missionaries got more involved. My colleague, Allen Avery, had funds that could be used for income-generating projects. We tried multiple projects that failed, such as supplying families of church leaders with knitting yarn to make things for sale, or with small sums of money to help them open small businesses. All of this was in an effort to help mature Christians survive in rural areas and continue leading their churches. Not a single leader lived on support in our rural churches, so all had to make a living some way.

Isaac in his cotton field.

Meanwhile there was a tremendous brain drain of talent leaking out of Zimbabwe. Anyone with ambition or skills headed out of Zimbabwe for the greener pastures of places like South Africa and Botswana in search of better job opportunities. Even rural leaders with limited education were tempted to abandon not only churches but also families to make a better living as the Zimbabwean economy plunged into never-ending recession. Many did succeed at making a better living by moving out, but often at great cost to their closest relationships and to their own spiritual lives.

Who Needs a Missionary?

Cotton proved to be something of an answer to the conundrum of how to make a decent living in rural parts of Zimbabwe. Matabeleland North turned out to be ideal for growing cotton, so Allen began to provide loans to help church leaders get started. He gave them just enough loan money to buy seeds, fertilizer, insecticide and sprayers, and let them use their existing farm implements, which were usually animal-drawn plows and handheld hoes.

Whereas other loan projects failed, cotton succeeded marvelously in the Binga District. Church leaders there not only got a harvest but were also able to sell it to Cottco, the Cotton Company of Zimbabwe, which sent trucks to collect the bales. They made enough money to repay the loans, with some left over for family needs. Finally, a project that worked out!

Yet cotton farming was intense hard work and it proved dangerous too. As the cotton crop matured, it attracted elephants who like to eat cotton bolls. Elephants were used to raiding Tonga fields in the months from February to May to help themselves to whatever grew there. As a result, the Tongas would often live in the fields during those months to guard their crops. Some would tie strips of plastic on long strings around the borders of their fields to try to confuse the pachyderms, but usually to no avail.

Isaac showed me the shelters his people built in the fields, essentially elevated platforms with a thatched roof where they could sleep lightly in order to hear the elephants at night. They would cook meals in the shade of the platforms during the day. Isaac showed me how they slept in a sitting position with arms around their legs and head on their knees, so that they could not fall into deep sleep when on guard duty.

Tongas have an acute sense of hearing, which Isaac demonstrated when we were awaiting our return bus to Bulawayo after our visit in 1989. We bedded down in a church building near the main road in the evening to wait for our bus to arrive at around 2:00 am. We needed no alarm clock as Isaac did his light sleeping routine and awakened us, saying he could hear the bus coming. Assuming the bus was almost at our stop, we scampered around to get over to the road with our luggage, but it was fully another ten to fifteen minutes before we could hear the bus at all. How Isaac had heard it from so far away remains a mystery to me.

Since the Tongas were not allowed to own firearms, their only resort when elephants invaded their fields at night was to use noise, sticks, and stones in an attempt to frighten them away. No doubt it was also frightening to the Tongas to engage such monsters in the dark. More than a few

Tongas were killed each year in these pitched battles for food. Isaac told me about a young Tonga mother with a baby tied to her back who was not only attacked and killed by an angry elephant, but also buried! In its rage, the elephant actually dug a hole in the ground and shoved the woman and baby in it.

Isaac himself was almost killed in a field one day as he challenged an elephant for ownership of some pumpkins. He was armed with stones but the elephant charged him. The only advantage an unarmed man has with an elephant is that his small size makes it easier to dodge around obstacles, for he cannot outrun the massive creature. Isaac survived by zigzagging out of the elephant's line of charge into a sharp turn around some bushes that the elephant couldn't make. Some trees and river banks then gave him protection.

It was not elephants that almost put Isaac out of the cotton business, however, but the uneven playing field of globalized business. After several good years of cotton farming, which enabled Isaac to construct a brick house for his family and buy a two-wheeled animal-drawn cart called a scotch cart, the world price of cotton fell so far that it no longer paid for all the back-breaking cultivation and the uncertainty of elephant raids. The Tongas did everything by hand, reaping the cotton and stuffing it into giant two-hundred kilogram bales. The process often dirtied the cotton, making it a lower grade.

Isaac and Margaret with their family in front of a cotton bale.

True, part of the reason for the collapse of the cotton market had to do with Zimbabwe's government policies, which made fuel difficult to obtain for the Cottco trucks that collected the bales, and the prevailing lawlessness that allowed crooks to swindle lots of cotton farmers in gin towns like Gokwe. Getting paid for the cotton crop was a hazardous occupation in itself.

Once a year, following the harvest, the peasant farmers would travel to Gokwe for a paycheck. For them, it was an unimaginable amount of money to get all at once, like winning the lottery, except that it had come from an entire season's labor. For many Tongas there was a strong temptation to celebrate with their pockets full of money, and Gokwe willingly provided bars and prostitutes, as well as plenty of con artists trying to part the peasants from their hard-earned cash. Gokwe became something of a wild-West kind of town, with the farmers often on the losing end of bad deals.

But the other dominant reason for the worldwide fall of cotton prices has to do with United States and European government policies that protect and subsidize their own cotton farmers in order to keep out cheaper cotton from the non-Western world. Robert Guest, correspondent for the *Economist* magazine, wrote in his book *The Shackled Continent* that the wealthier nations could pay much less for agricultural products if they would merely open up their markets to places like Africa. Yet Western governments choose to protect and enrich their own farmers with taxpayer money at the expense of non-Western farmers. Guest noted, "Farm subsidies in rich countries are running at about a billion dollars a day. That is roughly equivalent to the entire GDP of sub-Saharan Africa. African farmers simply cannot compete."[2] He concluded that Western protectionism costs poor nations $100 billion a year, which is twice what they receive in aid.[3] Globalization has proved not to be a level playing field, despite the world supposedly being "flat." Official government subsidies by the richest nations, which often claim to follow free market principles, have cost African cotton farmers millions of jobs. Isaac's was one of them; although he could always return to cotton farming for part of his income, he could not make a living through cotton alone.

Next he tried selling dried fish to a soldiers' camp in Kwekwe. This demanded a trip to Mujele to procure the fish, load them on a bus, and travel about two hundred miles one way to reach the town of Kwekwe where there was a ready market for dried fish. The soldiers would buy on credit,

---

2. Guest, *The Shackled Continent*, 165.
3. Ibid., 166.

necessitating follow-up visits to collect what was owed. When the soldiers began insisting that Sunday was their best day to meet him to square up accounts, he realized that this business was taking away his actual calling. He needed to be in Magobbo to preach on Sundays. After three weeks of this effort, he quit.

His next project was to sell clothes to the fishermen of Mujele, but the same problem occurred. The fishermen also wanted credit, and wanted him to collect debts on Sundays. Clearly the Christian heritage of Zimbabwe's colonial days has made Sunday the universal day off. But that is not so for a preacher of the gospel. After two weeks he quit this project as well.

Now Isaac turned back to his main asset: his herd of cattle. Back when he first started to preach in Magobbo, we searched for ways to help him support his family. We came up with an idea to supply him just two cattle as the nucleus of a future herd. All over Africa, cattle are the main way of creating and saving family wealth. Rarely will Africans butcher a cow for consumption, as cows bear calves and yield nutritious milk. A herd is the banking system, as the owners can build the herd to increase their prosperity or sell cattle in time of need. The so-called "bride price" or *lobola* was traditionally paid in cattle as a means of cementing ties between the bride's and groom's families.

Isaac was very pleased at the suggestion of receiving two cattle. Our sponsoring church in Santa Ana, California, Northside Church of Christ (now Journey Christian Church in Irvine), undertook to raise the funds for the animals. With typical zest, Bill and Mary Cliff, aided by J. T. and Blanca Johnson, spurred our support team on and came up with the funds. But there was a catch: Isaac's area of Magobbo had been without cattle for a long time because of the tsetse fly, which had only recently been eradicated and which causes certain death to livestock. The nearest cattle available for purchase were about a hundred miles away near the Catholic mission of Kariyangwe.

Armed with cash, Isaac boarded a bus for Kariyangwe and bought two young cattle as a breeding pair. What happened next has never ceased to amaze me. Isaac and a helper or two drove the two animals to Magobbo walking the entire hundred miles on foot! They carried only maize meal to cook and some water to drink over the blistering Zambezi valley that teemed with wild animals. Such an adventure would never have occurred to me to undertake, but for the Tongas, it was just how one did business. After several days of walking and sleeping around a campfire at night, Isaac had his cattle back home.

Who Needs a Missionary?

Isaac tending to his first small herd of cattle.

Each time I visited Isaac, which was not frequent due to the remoteness of his home, I would ask how many cattle he now had. He constructed a large corral near his house and his sons became herders as is common in African families. After milking the cows with calves early each morning, the boys would take the herd out to find pasture and water for the day, and bring them back in the evening. Traditionally, this is how young African boys spend their days, developing bush skills along the way.

When we had a missionary apprentice, Mark Elefritz, with us, he decided to tag along with a herd boy named Letshane to see what he did all day in the bush country in Tsholotsho District. Besides knowing where to find water and grass, Letshane let Mark see one amazing skill he had. Ndebele herd boys carry a knobkerrie, or *induku*, as both protection and weapon. It is the traditional warrior's weapon, a strong stick about a meter long with a knob on one end that can be used like a club. Letshane spotted a dove in a tree and hurled his knobkerrie at it, neatly popping its head clean off! Letshane and Mark then enjoyed a lunch of roasted dove that day.

As Isaac's sons brought in the herd each evening, I counted around forty head of cattle that came from that original pair. Isaac always knew the exact number, giving his cattle names that described them fondly. It must be with great satisfaction that the head of the family sees the dust rising from his herd as it approaches the family kraal in the evening. The fading twilight becomes hazy with the dust and musical with the tinkling cowbells as the herd comes home.

Some decades later, Isaac was able to use his herd to start a new business. Noticing that a mysterious cow disease was striking some of his neighbors' cattle that wandered into the forest, he realized it might be the right time to sell off a few head. He discussed the situation with his son Moses, who was in his late teens. The two agreed to go into the welding business, but they needed to buy a welding machine and generator. They would operate in the Siabuwa business center as the only welding business for fifty miles if they could swing it. But a few obstacles remained: how to procure the equipment and bring it back, and how to ensure a supply of diesel since the nearest gas station was in Binga, fifty miles away. The diesel was necessary to run the generator, as Siabuwa was not yet on Zimbabwe's electric grid. If their risky venture succeeded, they would be the sole welders between Binga and Gokwe!

Isaac sold eight cattle to a Shona businessman in order to fund his new investments. The businessman offered to take Moses with him to the capital city of Harare to obtain the welding machine and generator with the money from the sale of the cattle. Moses had never been that far from home and after he had been gone five days, Isaac became anxious about him. Fortunately, as Isaac started out towards Harare to look for Moses, he found him on his way home with all the equipment and some change to spare!

In 2010, father and son launched the welding business both in Siabuwa repairing scotch carts and installing burglar bars in shops and homes, and on Lake Kariba repairing fishing boats. Isaac currently wants to expand into building and selling scotch carts so he is still trying to raise capital for that. As a result he has continued to grow cotton in small quantities in order to inject more capital into the welding business. In 2010, at the time of the early harvest, Cottco was offering a mere thirty cents per kilogram or around sixty dollars per two-hundred kilogram bale of cotton, but doubled that offer in mid-year. Isaac harvested only five bales and had to sell the first two at the low price in order to keep his welding business afloat. Whenever he needs diesel to run the generator, Moses must board a bus to Binga, spending a whole day to buy and bring back the fuel. Doing business in Siabuwa is challenging to say the least!

Clearly, Isaac has an entrepreneurial aptitude and is willing to try all sorts of things to make a living. Along the way, he is also training his sons in business practices as he himself discovers what will work, and what won't. Few rural church leaders are as creative as he is in finding ways to support his family, but he is determined to be self-supporting and teaches his younger disciples to do the same. He is also careful not to let business get in the way of ministry, and when it does, he drops that business opportunity.

One reason Isaac is so concerned about conducting business to support his family is that this lifestyle increases his credibility as an evangelist and pastor. Knowing Isaac's connection with white missionaries, Tongas would ask him if he received a salary for preaching, and he would reply, "No, I don't preach for money." They couldn't understand why and assumed that whenever he would travel to Bulawayo for a church meeting, he must rendezvous with missionaries to get a paycheck. So Isaac started paying for others to accompany him to the city to see for themselves what went on. First he paid for Mpendulo, his cousin, to attend a church meeting, and later he funded others. Sometimes those people would receive something at the meeting, such as one man who was given a pair of shoes by Janelle Avery, but upon returning home they would testify that Isaac did not get paid on these trips. Isaac's motto was and is, "I will get paid in heaven."

The Basis for Bivocational Ministry

In many parts of the world, there is a definite need for bivocational ministry. This is not a new concept, as it began with the early apostles. While the New Testament gives fulltime church workers the right to receive a salary, that right was not always taken. The apostle Paul explains why in 1 Corinthians 9:3-18. He admits that he has the right to be supported for his work as apostle, using such memorable phrases as "Who serves as a soldier at his own expense? Who plants a vineyard and does not eat of its grapes? Who tends a flock and does not drink of the milk?" (1 Cor 9:7). He quotes an Old Testament passage about not muzzling the ox as it treads out the grain, saying it certainly applies to church workers as well. Just as any hard-working farmer deserves to eat of the harvest, so a fulltime worker for the gospel has the right to financial support. But he adds that he had not used those rights in Corinth. Why not?

Paul inserts a consideration for the gospel that often caused him to forego his rights of support. He bluntly says, "We put up with anything rather than hinder the gospel of Christ" (1 Cor 9:12). Rather than create a possible impression that preaching the gospel is just a job, or just about

Making a Living

making money, Paul preferred to work with his own hands to make his living. He makes it clear that with or without a salary, he must preach the gospel, "for I am compelled to preach. Woe to me if I do not preach the gospel!" (1 Cor 9:16). He prefers to make his preaching free of charge so that questions about money do not arise when people wonder why he preaches.

We are not usually as careful with money as Paul was. As a result, a lot of our practices raise questions about money that are hard to answer with integrity. We assume that all fulltime preachers should be supported because that is our ideal at home. Therefore when we go to other countries where many preachers are not supported by their local congregations, we try to raise support for them elsewhere. Such actions almost always undermine the gospel itself, as non-Christians are made to believe that going into fulltime ministry is about making money through foreign support. In those places, people rush to sign up for jobs in preaching, thinking of the gospel ministry as a ticket to prosperity.

In my book, *Roots and Remedies of the Dependency Syndrome in World Missions*, I describe how Southern Baptists started their mission work in Zimbabwe in the 1950s by supporting every local pastor with foreign funds.[4] Before they had planted many churches or developed many local leaders, they founded a seminary to train pastors who understood that they would be provided jobs upon graduation. While this approach seemed productive and resulted in rapid church growth, it was not sustainable in the long run. Foreign funding could not keep up with the number of Zimbabweans who desired to be supported.

When the Baptist Mission executives realized that their system of hiring pastors was no longer feasible, they decided to turn over all support of pastors to local Zimbabwean congregations.[5] In 1960, a Ten Year Plan was implemented to phase out foreign support and introduce local support for all pastors, but the change sparked a rebellion of Zimbabwean church leaders against their missionaries. Pastors did not see how struggling new congregations could possibly pay them as regularly and as well as the Baptist Mission. The President of the Zimbabwean Baptist Convention made this statement at the 1964 annual meeting: "Whereas we have had showers of blessing in the past, today we are having showers of stones,"[6] referring primarily to the results of the Ten Year Plan.

---

4. Reese, *Roots and Remedies*, 65–75.
5. Ibid., 67.
6. Ibid., 68.

Who Needs a Missionary?

The effort to switch from foreign to local pay for pastors complicated the relationship between the Baptist Mission and the local church leaders for decades. Resentment boiled over into hostility on occasion. For example, a disgruntled former pastor entered the civil service of Zimbabwe where he was able to convince the Department of Immigration to deny Baptist missionaries new work permits because of his remaining resentment over the Ten Year Plan. This ex-pastor was "instrumental in reducing Southern Baptist missionaries on the field from thirty-four [family] units down to only nine"[7] during the mid-1990s.

No doubt the model with which Southern Baptists began their mission work was flawed and it has since been abandoned. Regular infusions of American money to support local pastors tempted many unsuitable people to enter the ministry for the perceived material benefits. So why did the Southern Baptists initially assume American money was needed to support pastors for new congregations? Reflection on the early history of the Southern Baptist Convention would have offered a more appropriate model. The earliest Baptist pastors on the American frontier were bivocational and not seminary-trained. Yet church growth was still rapid and widespread, especially during the Second Great Awakening. Nathan Hatch explained how simple preachers from the Methodist and Baptist churches spread Christianity so rapidly that they came to represent "two-thirds of the Protestant ministers and church members in the United States."[8] This mass movement democratized Christianity on the frontier, undermining the influence of older denominations that continued to rely solely on seminary-trained pastors.

Zimbabwe in the 1950s and even today resembles the American frontier in many respects. The fastest growing churches do not depend on seminary-trained pastors nor provide every graduate with a salary from overseas. That is simply not feasible, healthy, or biblical. Roland Allen knew this fact almost a century ago and wrote about it in books such as *Voluntary Clergy* (1923) and *The Case for a Voluntary Clergy* (1930). Even then, the production of seminary-trained pastors could not keep pace with church needs in Britain or anywhere else.

Allen was a missionary for the Anglican Church in China, and certainly his church upheld high educational standards for its priests. But along with that elaborate training went an expectation for a salary provided

---

7. Ibid., 74–75.
8. Hatch, *Democratization of American Christianity*, 3.

Making a Living

by the church. Allen wrote, "In India, China, and Africa no man is ordained unless he is dependent for his livelihood upon a clerical salary."[9] Allen, however, did not see this model of leadership training in the New Testament. He lamented, "We abandoned the Apostolic conception of the ministry; we find that we have abandoned the Apostolic conception of the Church."[10]

Pragmatically, Allen found the system of providing foreign salaries for church workers in mission areas to be too expensive and unproductive. In addition, foreign salaries inadvertently divided church workers into two levels: "Very early the native Christian community was divided into two classes, workers who were called mission agents and the rest who were not."[11] Mature workers who did not receive salaries were thus downgraded simply for not being chosen, yet they were often more productive in ministry. Allen understood that being paid a salary from a foreign source actually made a worker less productive, saying that the paid worker "is financially dependent upon the mission. . . . In relation to his own people, or his congregation, he feels no responsibility to them, and they feel no responsibility for him."[12]

As soon as salaries are offered, having access to money becomes the focus of ministry. Allen said that the system of paid church workers teaches Christians that "all growth depends on money."[13] Not only does this system attract the wrong people to ministry but it also corrupts those who have good motives to begin with. We saw that in our ministry in Zimbabwe. Being a tiny mission, we had no big sums of money to dispense, so very few ever got salaries from us. But those who did were never as productive as others who did not receive pay, with Isaac being the prime example. Furthermore, some who received salaries became corrupted by it and started dreaming of ways to get their hands on as much mission money as they could, to the extent of undermining the entire mission if need be.[14] Killing the goose that laid the golden egg was not uncommon in the end.

---

9. Allen, *Voluntary Clergy*, 26.
10. Ibid., 72.
11. Allen, *Case for Voluntary Clergy*, 34.
12. Ibid., 209.
13. Ibid., 212.
14. Reese, *Roots and Remedies*, 79–82.

Summary

Every Christian worker has to decide what to do about support. Some seem to assume that churches should always support them if they want to be fulltime workers. In many parts of the world, Bible colleges seem to be a ticket to a steady job. Drawing a salary for doing God's work is certainly permissible, but that may not be the best approach to ministry. Paul sometimes accepted donations from churches, but did not count on receiving them in order to make a living. He was concerned that people might think that gospel work is like any regular job, or that Christian ministry is about making money. In some cases, a "tentmaking" kind of job may create more credibility for ministry than fulltime support.

If we think that money drives all mission work, we will wonder how Isaac could be more productive than someone on a regular salary. But remember that Isaac never asked for a salary, desiring the maximum integrity for his indigenous ministry. In this, he was just like the apostle Paul, even though he probably didn't realize the similarity. It was just the same as Paul's instinct not to devalue the gospel message by associating it with a salary. And that is why Isaac was also more productive, because the task of spreading the gospel became very personal between him and his Savior. He remains accountable to the Lord as well as to the people he preaches to. He deeply needed that personal relationship in order to face the waves of obstacles that he would encounter in ministry.

5

Obstacles and Suffering

As if making a living for one's family was not enough of a hurdle on its own, Isaac also faced additional obstacles to his ministry. Some came from health problems, some from opponents, and some from the devil himself. In fact, in African cultures there is no real distinction between physical and spiritual illnesses or calamities. Everything is spiritual in the end. While our Western mind likes to categorize obstacles into various headings, the African mind would lump them all into spiritual obstacles that cause suffering.

The first problem arose as soon as Isaac arrived in Magobbo with his family in 1987. He came with his new Ndebele wife, Margaret, and three small children: Nomsa, Lazarus, and Moses. They all got sick immediately, probably with malaria as it was the rainy season. Coming from Bulawayo, which is not a malaria zone, they had not developed the Tonga resistance to this disease that comes with repeated bouts.

In true African form, the Tongas concluded that Isaac's family would all die soon, because Ndebele people were not supposed to be in that area. Ancestral spirits are seen as territorial and obviously Margaret and her children were a long way from their ancestral home. Isaac's response to this thought was, "Jesus is still here despite the illness." He told his neighbors that he had not stolen Margaret from her parents, and the children were his legitimately. They had every right to live in the Zambezi valley.

As Margaret in particular got worse and worse, Isaac took her and the children to the Siabuwa clinic where Dr. Chineka advised him to take them all to Bulawayo as quickly as possible in order to remove them from the malaria zone and get urgent treatment. Isaac took them by bus to town.

When they arrived, Margaret was too ill to walk, so he hired a taxi to get his family to his uncle's house in Pelandaba suburb.

With Allen Avery's help, Isaac got his whole family admitted to Bulawayo Central Hospital. After he informed his in-laws in Chief Sigola's area just outside town about the serious illness, his mother-in-law came to the hospital to look after Margaret and the children. This allowed Isaac to think about returning to his fields in Magobbo. With Margaret's blessing he left to attend to his fields so his family would have food when they returned home. He found that his new converts had already harvested most of the crops for him. Many non-Christian neighbors, however, predicted that Margaret would never come back with the children. Imagine their surprise when she soon reappeared! Margaret would get seriously ill with malaria and asthma again, but as of this writing in 2013, she is still living in the Zambezi valley and has made the difficult adjustment to life in a malaria zone.

In those early days, trials mounted like waves on an angry ocean. Isaac brought four chickens from the Wolhuters' chicken farm to start a flock. The flock grew to fourteen hens that first year. When Allen Avery came to visit him and to check on Margaret's health, Isaac went to get a chicken for the pot, but found that all fourteen adult hens had mysteriously died. The lone rooster was left to keep the chicks. This incident got the neighbors' tongues wagging again. Their verdict was that Isaac had narrowly avoided losing his family and now had lost all his breeding chickens in one day. Clearly his ancestral spirits were angry with him for not following Tonga customs. Isaac quietly buried the dead chickens and then was criticized for not letting people eat them!

Even cases of church benevolence backfired against Isaac. For example, during one of the frequent droughts in Zimbabwe, American churches sent funds to buy maize seeds to distribute to needy church members. It so happened that the only type of seed available that year was popularly known as "Kenya" maize, actually American yellow corn provided by the US government. Zimbabweans could not ordinarily stomach Kenya corn and were only willing to do so during droughts. On top of their usual aversion to the yellow corn meal, this particular batch of seeds happened to be infested with weevils all through the ninety-kilogram sacks. People complained to Isaac so much about the donated seeds that he asked Allen to stop sending seeds to Magobbo.

When his former bosses, Geoff and Sandy Wolhuter, came to visit him soon after he settled at Magobbo, they brought two fifty-kilogram bales

Obstacles and Suffering

of used clothing, telling him he could distribute them to needy folks in the church. That also became a problem for Isaac. In a church with mostly women, it easily appeared to their non-Christian husbands that Isaac was trying to seduce the women by giving them clothes! To avoid the appearance of any impropriety, he prayed for the wisdom of Solomon and got an idea: he hung all of the clothing on a long rope between two trees and told the church members to pick one item that they wanted. Now he was not singling out an item of clothing for an individual, but was letting them choose for themselves, so avoiding any misunderstandings.

During this time, Isaac was staying with his maternal uncle, James Siajeya, who was a traditional healer or *inyanga*. This living arrangement brought its own obstacles to the budding ministry. Isaac no longer followed the age-old beliefs of his ancestors, and people were beginning to accuse him of forsaking Tonga culture. That was not just considered an unfortunate decision an individual might make; it was much more ominous, as it potentially brought the whole community into peril. Isaac's decision to follow Christ and to persuade as many as possible to join him and his family was viewed as a direct challenge to the ancestral spirits who might at any time lash out against the community. And the clash between Christianity and traditional African religion began right at home!

One evening Isaac was praying with his family when another member of the extended family named Maria collapsed in her house with a bout of demon possession. Siajeya went to see what was bothering his daughter-in-law and was told that Maria had met with an evil spirit. He gathered his *inyanga* paraphernalia to tend to her, while Isaac continued praying in his own hut despite hearing the commotion. He realized that people felt he was betraying their customs and he knew he needed God's help through prayer. Siajeya brought a wildebeest's tail to be used to sprinkle *muthi* (traditional medicine) from a gourd and a wooden plate. He was about to begin his incantations when Isaac walked in to see Maria kicking around on the floor.

Sizing up the situation, Isaac laid hands on Maria and prayed, "Thank you, Jesus, that you are here." He prayed for Maria's deliverance from the evil spirit and it was soon expelled without the need for traditional healing. Siajeya was quite surprised that demons could come out through prayer to Jesus alone. That was the first of many demons that Isaac had to deal with at home as he began his ministry, and he did it right in front of Siajeya.

At one of the early church services shortly after that incident, Isaac was praying for the sick when an outbreak of demon possession hit the

Who Needs a Missionary?

group. Seven people fell down at one time. Isaac attributes this spectacle to the widespread understanding that he was no longer following Tonga customs, so people with issues stemming from evil spirits were coming to church to see what he might do, or to test him. Now Isaac wondered how he could possibly pray for all these demonized people at once; some were running away from the meeting, while others were writhing on the ground like snakes. Isaac prayed, "Jesus, you sent me to be a light to this place. Here are your people who need freedom. I don't have the power to free them. Those who are running away, let them stop."

Amazingly, all the demonized people stopped and stayed still, giving Isaac time to pray for them one by one. All of them were miraculously delivered. Now Isaac's reputation grew as someone who could free people from evil spirits. But the Tongas were also suspicious of him as someone who no longer followed the traditions of the ancestors. They still came to him for deliverance from evil spirits but secretly believed he would eventually return to worshipping *amadlozi* (ancestral spirits).

Another obstacle that proved to be continuous for years came from the fact that, like most Christian evangelists around the world, Isaac was more successful at winning women to Christ than men. His wife, Margaret, never complained about his work for Christ or his witnessing to women. She supported him fully and continues to do so. But non-Christian Tonga men accused Isaac of trying to seduce their wives in the name of Jesus.

Like most Africans who follow traditional religion, Tongas brewed beer from maize as part of ancestor worship. In Tonga custom, the wife would test to see if the beer was ready. If it was, she would take a spoonful of it to her husband's hut, kneel outside, and hand it to the man who would be kneeling inside. He would then pour it out as a libation to the spirits, performing *ukuthethela* rituals. When wives became Christians, however, they refused to take part in these rituals or to tend to the beer. Men came to regard Isaac as evil and anti-social for his role in turning their wives against ancient customs that they considered essential to the group well-being. Isaac responded with more fasting and prayer.

His most severe test in this area arose from what had been one of his most notable successes as an evangelist. Back in 1989, when Mark Elefritz and I were visiting Magobbo, we spent some time in the neighboring village of Chisale almost daily talking to the old man, Chilawela, as described in Chapter 3. Every night we could hear drumming and dancing coming from the direction of Chilawela's kraal. His son, Joseph, was an *iwosana*, a

Obstacles and Suffering

rainmaker, and people desiring good rains were singing and dancing into the wee hours, praising Joseph as the man who could make it happen!

One of the unique aspects of spending a night in an African village is that you will often hear the sound of drums and singing late at night. Sound carries a long way in the night air and, as long as it is not too close, the sound of drums is an oddly satisfying African experience. Perhaps because white folks have so little rhythm, we can appreciate those who do. The source of the music and the reason for late-night singing and dancing, however, often escape us. Many times it has to do with ancestral spirit worship or the spirits in general, and the drinking and dancing are designed to induce spirit possession in order to receive a message from them. All of that, however, does not reduce the attractiveness of the music itself. African traditional religion is highly addictive and lots of fun at first, until the next day when *ibabalazi* (hangover) sets in.

I asked Isaac about the music and he explained that Joseph claimed to have *muthi* that a person could place around the borders of a field to make it rain on that field. The praise singers who gathered at Joseph's home each evening treated him like a superstar, making fantastic claims about his prowess in rainmaking. They said he could actually cause rain to fall on your field (for a price) and not on your neighbor's field. They added that he could elephant-proof your field, preventing the mammoths from entering and feasting on your crops so nicely provided by his rain. So the music we were hearing regularly was nothing more than a false advertising campaign, designed to lead people into the adoration of a mere man. At the time, I remember thinking what a difficult place Isaac had chosen to minister, but Joseph was Chilawela's son, and Isaac would soon baptize the elderly man.

Once Chilawela was a Christian, Isaac had an inroad into the rest of the family. Joseph would be a hard nut to crack, of course, because he had so much invested in his reputation as an *iwosana*. Not for nothing was Joseph known as *Kanubwaila*, a Tonga word meaning one who stalks an unsuspecting man. He also knew nothing about Christianity, so Isaac fasted about how to approach him with the gospel. The opening came when Joseph's wife, Betina, responded to the gospel.

Betina was a crippled woman, and Isaac would visit her whenever Joseph was at home so he could also preach to him. Joseph did not agree to follow his wife in being a Christian, but after some time sent Isaac word through Betina, saying, "I am ashamed of coming to church as my followers will wonder about me." Isaac responded by offering to come and get him for the church service, and that is how Joseph also started worshipping the true God.

Eventually, Isaac took Joseph and Betina and their children to live with him. Since they had become Christians, their rainmaking income ceased; Betina was crippled and Joseph was diabetic. Now they depended on Isaac to feed them. In that way, Joseph's children became familiar with Isaac's home, almost like his own children. So it came as a shock to Isaac when he was accused by some of Joseph's family of impregnating his daughter, Maud, after she had grown up! This scandal was to be one of the most severe tests Isaac would face, as it drew in key church leaders from Bulawayo to investigate. I only heard about the issue from Allen Avery, who led a delegation of church leaders to Magobbo, as by that time we no longer lived in Zimbabwe.

What led up to this serious allegation? Some years before the accusations against Isaac were made, Maud told Isaac that she had found a husband from Mashonaland, whom she had met when he came to buy some chickens from her father. Maud even said she was already preparing to pack up and leave for the man's home, so Isaac asked to meet him. When he arrived, Isaac asked him his intentions towards Maud, and he confirmed that he intended to marry her. Isaac then advised, "You must allow her to worship God at your home." Sadly, the man did not take Maud home with him as she expected, but left her standing at the Siabuwa bus stop while he ran off alone.

Humiliated, Maud returned home and stopped coming to church services; it was soon discovered that she was pregnant. Her father Joseph died around that time, so other relatives asked her who the father of her child was, and she named the man from Mashonaland. Eventually a baby boy was born to Maud and five years went by before her relatives brought charges against Isaac, claiming that he was the real father. By then, Betina had also died, leaving family leadership entirely in the hands of non-Christians. They did not present their charges to Isaac face-to-face, but instead approached some church leaders at Kalonga who worked closely with Isaac, since he had helped plant the church there. Isaac's co-workers, Jaison Tshuma and Phambanisa Mutale, then conveyed the charges to Isaac when he came to worship at Kalonga.

The Tonga rule in such cases is that once a charge of impregnating an unmarried woman is made, her parents or relatives usually chase the woman away to go and live with the accused man. They then seek "damages" from the man to repay the family for making their daughter unfit for marriage to anyone else. They also expect him to pay a bride price in order to marry and care for her from then on, even if he already has a wife, as polygamy is considered normal.

For a while, the Magobbo village headman protected Isaac, but Maud's family threatened to take him to court as well. Eventually, court police arrived at Isaac's home to deliver a summons. Accompanied by two of his closest co-workers, Faison Mudenda and Francis Mudimba, both of whom were also his converts, Isaac went to the Chisale village court where Maud's family lived near Magobbo. In his own defense, Isaac asked two main questions: "How old is the boy you accuse me of fathering?" And when they admitted he was five years old, he asked, "Why did you wait five years to accuse me? It should be something new you are accusing me of doing."

Isaac then turned to Maud herself, who was present at the court. He asked her to speak up with what she knew, but she remained quiet for a while. Then she started sobbing and her relatives told her to stop crying. Isaac then asked the relatives, "Where did I meet with Maud in order to do what you accuse me of doing?" "In your house, of course," they replied. "In which room? Maud knows all the rooms in my house," he countered. "We don't know, but the boy looks like you," they replied. Isaac then offered to submit to a blood test to determine if the boy was his son, but the relatives declined and insisted that the case should move forward to a higher court.

Shortly after this, Isaac's wife, Margaret, arrived from Bulawayo where she had been visiting her family. When she heard of all the accusations and court proceedings, she became angry with Maud's relatives. "We took members of their family in and fed them when times were hard, and look how they are repaying us," she said. She knew the accusations were false and wanted to go talk to the relatives about their charges.

Margaret and Isaac went along with Francis Mudimba to talk first to Maud. She revealed to them privately that her relatives had pressured her to name Isaac as her son's father in order to get his financial support and some security for their family. About that time, a delegation of church leaders including missionary Allen Avery and prominent leaders of Zimbabwe Christian Fellowship arrived, as they had heard about the charges. Isaac was not happy that they seemed to believe the accusations and he wanted to know who had informed them about the issue, but they refused to divulge that name.

Who Needs a Missionary?

Personally, I remember hearing from Allen about the charges and recall that Allen felt at the time that the allegations were a cause for serious concern. I felt sick in the bottom of my stomach to think that Isaac had succumbed to sexual temptation, and how adversely this would affect not only his own family and flock but all the sister congregations too. We had known other leaders who had committed the sin mentioned in Malachi 2:15 as "breaking faith with the wife of your youth." Enormous harm is always done by the wrongful actions of one man who leads a group of Christians; the repercussions are not only immediate but long-term too. When a prominent leader betrays his wife, it lowers the standard for everyone in the future.

In Isaac's case, there was not much substance to the charges in the end, as his accusers were just an idle family hoping to profit by pressuring an innocent man. During the times I have visited Magobbo since this sad incident, I have never seen any further repercussions. Isaac's good name was restored following all the various investigations. Charges were dropped and nothing came of them, but they were certainly a test of his leadership at the time and they could easily have cost Isaac his whole ministry and reputation.

This prolonged fiasco was not the only obstacle that threatened to undo Isaac's ministry. Another episode that took place near the beginning of his work in Binga District posed a similar threat. This one involved fellow Christians and stemmed from a man named Gilbert Muzamba, who worshipped with the Assembly of God at Nagangala on the main road, where the primary school that served Isaac's family was located. When some problems arose in the Assembly of God congregation, Gilbert was looking around for another church to work with, and Isaac invited him to join his work.

I remember meeting Gilbert in Bulawayo not long after Isaac began his work at Magobbo. Gilbert seemed to have the makings of a good leader, as he already had experience in evangelism and in growing a church. Isaac paid Gilbert's way to Bulawayo twice so he could accompany him to meet with us and receive some of the training that we were doing with other leaders. Since my supporting churches in the USA had recently helped Isaac purchase two cattle as the nucleus of a potential herd, Allen decided to help Gilbert do the same. We treated Gilbert as if he had been part of our ministry team for a long time.

Obstacles and Suffering

Gilbert and Isaac returned to Binga District, and soon after that Gilbert's wife went to her parents' home at Jambezi near Victoria Falls to have a baby. Later, Isaac went back to Bulawayo for a leaders' meeting and Bible school that lasted most of a week. While he was away, his wife Margaret witnessed the Assembly of God splitting the Magobbo Church by taking the entire youth section and moving them only a short distance away to a newly constructed mud-hut type of building. From there the youths sang songs aimed at Isaac's flock, singing, "You are lost; come over here." I remember seeing the rival building and marveling that it was only a few hundred yards from Isaac's structure and very similar to it. Perhaps the most painful aspect of the whole episode was that it separated Isaac from Francis Mudimba, one of his first and most promising converts, who was still in high school at the time, but who was like a son to Isaac. The Assembly of God took his entire youth group with the exception of his own children.

You will recall that Isaac was not a well-educated person and he had come to rely on younger men who were; now those bright youngsters were suddenly stripped away from his influence. Francis was doing well in school and was becoming one of Isaac's best assistants at Magobbo.

Isaac's growing church in 1989. Mark is at the back right.

Who Needs a Missionary?

Isaac returned home to find this sad situation, but he blamed himself, wondering what he had done wrong. He decided to head back to town to report what had happened to Allen Avery. Allen responded that Isaac ought to insist the youth return to their home church immediately, but Isaac said he couldn't do that. This situation dragged on for quite some time, during which Allen would ask Isaac for an update whenever he saw him, but Isaac would reply, "I am still examining myself." Allen would reply, "But people are dying!" Isaac responded, "If a child leaves a father, then the father is the one who made a mistake."

After several months, the truth of what happened was revealed. Gilbert Muzamba had gone to the Assembly of God Church in Hwange, a coal-mining town, telling them he was restarting an Assembly of God at his home in Nagangala. He received papers to that effect from Pastor Simon Mukolo, the main leader of the Assembly of God there. Gilbert also took the names of all the youths who defected from Isaac to Pastor Mukolo, telling him he had also started a new branch of the Assemblies in Magobbo. It was he who instigated the mass defection of youths, as he had been meeting secretly with them to draw them away, including Francis who became a strong worker for the Assembly of God. Francis went to high school in Hwange which was a center for the Assemblies, so he became deeply involved with that group instead of Isaac's work.

Even when Isaac knew that Gilbert was the source of the division in his own church, he did not divulge this to Allen. Once when he took Gilbert to Emakhandeni for some training that we provided, Allen asked if the youth problem at Magobbo had been resolved, and Isaac simply replied that he was still waiting and praying for a solution. Later during this trip the two Tongas were together with Allen and me at my house, and there Isaac revealed that Gilbert had betrayed him by delivering the names of his entire youth group to the Assembly of God in Hwange, but Gilbert denied any knowledge of the issue at first. When pressed on the point, however, he finally acknowledged splitting the Magobbo Church.

Allen then told Gilbert to go and tell the youth to return to Isaac's church, but Gilbert replied that he couldn't do it right away since his wife was about to give birth in Jambezi, and he needed to go there first. Allen then gave Gilbert money to travel to Jambezi, return to Bulawayo to get a study book that he needed, and then go to Siabuwa to repair the damage he had caused. He also added money for diapers for the new baby. Gilbert simply took the money, went to Jambezi, and never showed up in Siabuwa

Obstacles and Suffering

again, making Jambezi his home. As the Tongas and other Africans say, he "ate" all the money Allen gave him, including the funds for the purchase of cattle. Isaac only saw Gilbert once more at an Assembly of God conference, where Isaac flatly told Gilbert he was a thief of God's money. He reported that Gilbert wept and the two men prayed together. Within two months Gilbert died in Jambezi.

In addition to the numerous betrayals and accusations, Isaac also had to withstand physical ailments, some of which threatened his ability to make a living. He lived in a harsh environment where the possibility of injury or disease was ever present. One day out in his field, he scratched his hand on something, but thought little of it at first. By the next day, however, his hand was severely swollen. His neighbors saw this and told him that his devotion to Jesus had caused this outcome, as he was upsetting the Tonga ancestral spirits. As his whole right arm became swollen and dark with poison from his hand to his armpit, he also began to wonder if his time to die had come.

He told Margaret, his wife, that he was going to the clinic at Siabuwa. When he got there, he tried to buy a Coca-Cola at a store, but collapsed in the doorway. He managed to get to the gate of the clinic where he met the nurse, MaGuchwa, who asked him what was wrong. By then the swelling extended beyond his arm down his right side. He told the nurse to cut the palm of his hand where the poison had started, but she refused. She called a doctor who did cut open his hand, letting out a stream of black blood. The doctor asked him if he had been bitten by something, but he was not aware of having been bitten, only scratched. Now a severe fever set in.

Isaac's fever spiked to an exceptionally high temperature and pills had no effect. The doctor wanted him to rush to Binga hospital, but Isaac had only five dollars in his pocket. By this time the fever had reached danger point. Isaac decided that he would wait for his wife to come with more money so they could pay the bus fare; he assured the doctor he didn't feel that bad. Margaret arrived with another fifteen dollars, but it was still not enough to pay for the bus, so the nurse contributed enough cash so both Isaac and Margaret could go together.

When they arrived at Binga District hospital, the first nurse they met backed away because of the putrid smell coming from Isaac's swollen arm. It smelled like a dead animal. The attending doctor was Dr. Gumbo, who gave Isaac tablets and injections to drive down the fever and fight the infection. The next morning a senior doctor arrived and suggested they take

Who Needs a Missionary?

Isaac to the larger hospital in Hwange in order to amputate the diseased arm. Dr. Gumbo did not agree, saying he would like to try to save the arm.

Dr. Gumbo's treatment consisted of cutting his right thumb on both sides to insert a tube into the arm. Soon, Isaac reported, both poisoned blood and rotten flesh started coming out of the tube. That did the job of removing the poison from his arm and he slowly began to heal. Once back home, his neighbors told him he needed to consult an *inyanga* and turn his back on the Jesus he had been following, but he refused all such suggestions. Certainly his hand was crippled and he was unable to use it for some time. I remember that he carried a small rubber ball with him to keep exercising his thumb and hand in order to regain his dexterity. Today his arm and hand have fully recovered and he can use them to do any manual labor essential for his farming and other work.

Some years later, just after my family moved out of Zimbabwe, Isaac again suffered from a mysterious illness that almost claimed his life. Even now, he says that he has never seen another disease like it, and neither had his doctors; it simply baffled everyone. He would sweat so much that his sheets became soaked and he couldn't eat, but his body temperature was normal. He became so dehydrated that he couldn't sit up or stand up and he had no saliva at all; he just slept.

Francis Mudimba, who had by this time been restored to partnership with Isaac after his temporary defection to the Assembly of God, came to visit Isaac. Seeing how seriously ill he was, Francis phoned Allen Avery to come urgently with a vehicle to transport Isaac to Binga hospital. Allen agreed to come immediately, estimating he would arrive by 2:00 pm the next day.

While waiting for Allen to arrive, Isaac drank water from a cup and asked for someone to read the Bible. This was during the cotton harvest in the spring, and his family had already received their annual check for their crop that had been delivered to the cotton gin. He asked Margaret to bring the check. When she did, he told her to deposit it so that if he should die, she would have access to the funds.

For the Bible reading, Isaac chose 2 Kings 20:1–11, the story of Hezekiah's near-death experience. Hezekiah became ill and was told by Isaiah, the prophet, to put his affairs in order, because he was about to die. Hezekiah responded by praying earnestly for God to spare his life. God answered by sending Isaiah back to tell him he would have fifteen more years to live. Putting himself in Hezekiah's place, Isaac said out loud to the people assembled in his house, "I am healed!" But there was no sign that the disease had left him; he was still sweating profusely. Still, Isaac took comfort from the Bible reading and reassured his wife and others that he would not die. While many gathered there doubted that he would live, he himself felt at peace.

Allen arrived on time that afternoon to find a lot of people gathered at Isaac's house. Isaac was so dehydrated that he could scarcely speak, and he tried to drink in order to communicate. Some of his family wanted an *inyanga* to come and throw bones to determine the cause of the illness, but he refused. Soon Allen had him at the Siabuwa clinic where they checked his vital signs. He still had no fever but was sweating and felt numb. Allen then took him on to Binga hospital where they admitted him; Margaret was permitted to sleep on the floor next to him.

Even in his hospital bed, Isaac remembers feeling sure that he would be healed as he recalled the verses of Hezekiah's story. For a whole week he could not eat, and was still unable to stand up, but his temperature was normal, so the medical team at the hospital had no idea how to treat the illness. His nurses concluded that he had an "African disease," probably emanating from the ancestral spirits, but he denied it. "I don't know how I will die," he told the nurses, "but this is not the disease that will kill me." To them, however, a disease that defied Western medical knowledge must come from spirits.

By this time, Allen had returned home to Bulawayo, leaving his phone number so the hospital staff could inform him if Isaac's situation changed. One day, Isaac ate an orange and was startled to find that his saliva suddenly returned. He immediately asked the staff to let him speak to Allen by phone. They marveled that he could even speak, but got in contact with Allen. Isaac simply told Allen that he was healed. Soon he was discharged from the hospital and went home. For some strange reason, which the doctors never discovered, as soon as he ate the orange he began to heal. From then on he was able to eat porridge and drink more liquids in order to regain his strength.

Although Isaac is healthy at the time of this writing, he has also experienced the loss of people close to him. These episodes were much more difficult for him to talk about, so details are not as numerous as for other issues we discussed so freely. We have referred to Francis Mudimba often in Isaac's story, because he was a convert, protégé, confidant, and relative of Isaac, even though the relationship was also clouded by his rejection of Isaac for a period during his teenage years. After being away at boarding

Who Needs a Missionary?

school in Hwange for his high school studies, Francis returned to Magobbo and became a teacher at Nagangala Primary School where Isaac's own children attended.

Gradually, Francis reintegrated himself into Isaac's work, after having been estranged from Isaac due to Gilbert Muzamba's influence. Now the bond that had been there before developed between the two men like that of father and son. Francis was a talented student and had the education that Isaac lacked, so they complemented each other. He was an avid reader, attended workshops in Bulawayo, and enjoyed traveling around to various churches to share his knowledge. As he matured into manhood and married, Francis became a trainer of others in discipleship. He continued to learn more himself and to pass on what he learned to newer disciples. In this way, he resumed his role as Isaac's right-hand man.

At a church meeting in Bulawayo, I am standing between Francis and Isaac.

In 2006, Francis became seriously ill. Isaac stayed by his side for seventeen days until he died. After that, Francis's brother moved from Magobbo to Kalonga with all the family's possessions. Soon rumors were spreading from Kalonga that Isaac had killed Francis by witchcraft, as he was jealous of Francis's rising position and education. Francis himself had denied that witchcraft caused his illness, but as he progressively got worse, he lost the ability to speak. In addition to suffering the loss of his best assistant, Isaac also bore the brunt of being somehow blamed for Francis's death.

But even worse than Francis's death was the death of Isaac's firstborn daughter, Nomsa, who succumbed to malaria. Nomsa was virtually the same age as our oldest daughter, Ellen, and the Wolhuters' oldest son, Jeremy. She was born June 12, 1980 while Isaac worked for the Wolhuters near Bulawayo. She reminded Isaac of his mother who had died on June 12, 1969. Nomsa moved with the family to Binga in 1987 and suffered numerous bouts of malaria along with her mother and siblings. But she survived those attacks and grew to be a young woman. She married and had Isaac and Margaret's first two grandchildren.

Nomsa contracted malaria at her home, but her husband was away working, so Isaac sent her to Binga hospital, as she was becoming anemic. She happened to arrive at the hospital during a doctors' strike; the first four days she received no treatment and died. She left behind a four-year-old boy and an eight-month-old girl. She was buried at Binga near the hospital. Although his family urged him to bring back soil from her tomb in accordance with Tonga custom, Isaac refused, saying Nomsa did not need two graves.

Despite the heartache that went along with the loss of his oldest daughter and his right-hand man, Isaac has persevered in ministry among his people. Despite regular rejection, accusations, family pressure, and suspicions, he has continued to train new leaders for ministry. He has not backed down from his beliefs, which shows how deeply he holds them. As a result, his ministry has remained fruitful, as he must depend solely on God for his own living and reputation. He has now become a seasoned leader, forged in the fires of adversity. This has always been the way God's leaders are shaped.

The Role of Suffering

No Christian usually goes looking for suffering, but it comes anyway. In fact, if men like Isaac had known how much it would cost to take the gospel to their own people, perhaps they would have declined to do it. But suffering always comes with the call to serve God. When Saul of Tarsus met Jesus face-to-face on the road to Damascus, he fell to the ground blinded by the light from heaven (Acts 9:8). Escorted into Damascus, he fasted for several days, waiting to find out what Jesus had in mind for him. God called a disciple in Damascus named Ananias to convey a message to Saul: "Go! This man is my chosen instrument to carry my name before the Gentiles and their kings and before the people of Israel. I will show him how much he must suffer for my name" (Acts 9:15–16).

Saul became the apostle Paul, and his itinerant ministry across the Roman world brought incredible suffering that few men could withstand. In 2 Corinthians 11:23–33, Paul describes his many afflictions for the sake of the gospel. He mentions beatings, dangers, hunger, exposure to the elements, and betrayal as standard treatment for an apostle of Christ. But he does not regret all this mistreatment. Rather he says, "I will boast of the things that show my weakness" (2 Cor 11:30). God even told him, "My grace is sufficient for you, for my power is made perfect in weakness" (2 Cor 12:8). Apparently, God prefers to put the valuable treasure of his gospel in earthen vessels that may sometimes crack or come close to it (2 Cor 4:7).

In Colossians 1:24, Paul makes an intriguing statement: "Now I rejoice in what was suffered for you, and I fill up in my flesh what is still lacking in regard to Christ's afflictions, for the sake of his body, which is the church." Part of Paul's understanding of Christian suffering is that it is always tied to Christ's. Without Jesus' suffering there would be no Christianity, so it is not considered by New Testament writers as incidental to either their faith or their work. Suffering is central to Christianity. There is always more to be experienced, and that is probably why Paul speaks of "what is still lacking in regard to Christ's suffering." The obvious difference between any evangelist's suffering and Christ's is that our Lord's is for atonement of sins; ours is merely the result of living in a fallen world filled with forces hostile to the gospel.

Peter dwelt on suffering at length in his first letter. As with Paul, it all related back to Jesus' suffering. Suffering then has a purpose, as it is sanctified by Christ (as long as the suffering is for living according to God's will). Peter says suffering refines a person's faith like fire does gold, so that faith "may be proved genuine and may result is praise, glory and honor when Jesus Christ is revealed" (1 Pet 1:7). For a dedicated servant of God, suffering is usually unjust, because the person is doing what God wants him or her to do. As long as it is not justified, suffering enters into the realm of what Jesus suffered for us. Peter says, "To this you were called, because Christ suffered for you, leaving you an example, that you should follow in his steps" (1 Pet 2:21). Jesus was insulted without retaliating and beaten without cursing his tormentors, trusting God instead to vindicate him in the end. As Jesus took the disgraceful treatment he received without complaining, so are we to react calmly to unjust punishment.

Peter used a text from Isaiah 8 regarding the response of faith to unfavorable events. Isaiah had just named his son Maher-Shalal-Hash-Baz according to God's instructions. The meaning of this ominous name—"quick to the plunder, swift to the spoil"—indicated that Assyria was about to invade Israel's northern kingdom and carry off its wealth. War was imminent, and Isaiah knew that the Assyrians would bring certain destruction on Syria and Samaria, and then would spill over into Judah, the southern kingdom of Israel. But God also warned Isaiah not to panic, but to keep living by faith in an uncertain time. God tells him in Isaiah 8:12: "Do not call conspiracy everything that these people call conspiracy; and do not fear what they fear."

Christian leaders need courage because fear can paralyze a person. Satan obviously uses fear to neutralize ministry efforts and he is often successful. The kind of courage required to withstand conspiracy theories and fearmongering is not brash but must be of supernatural origin. It goes along with "the peace that passes all understanding" (Phil 4:7). It arises from the confidence that God is in control and it seeks to do his will. As Peter says, it sets apart Jesus as Lord in order to give a solid reason for the hope we have in Christ (1 Pet 3:15). Such courage enables a person under pressure to answer critics with "gentleness and respect, keeping a clear conscience, so that those who speak maliciously against your good behavior in Christ may be ashamed of their slander" (1 Pet 3:16). The pressure that critics put us under should not distract us from the ultimate aim of presenting the gospel to them.

One aspect of Christianity in the global South that often differs markedly from traditional Christianity is its emphasis on the "prosperity gospel." Sociologist David Martin studied Latin American Pentecostalism extensively and made this observation:

> Pentecostalism has strong reservations about the European Christian approach to suffering as exemplary. It draws on indigenous Amerindian and black spiritual currents which have always flowed strongly beneath the surface of a colonial Catholicism and which regard suffering as something to be overcome.[1]

---

1. Martin, *Pentecostalism*, 75.

Who Needs a Missionary?

Martin noted that Pentecostalism in both Latin America and Africa often promotes the prosperity gospel: "It is a culture which positively celebrates material and physical goods as the Lord's blessings, especially the healed bodies and full tables which everywhere signal domestic comfort in place of *machista* chaos and waste."[2] On the other hand, Pentecostalism has "a pervasive suspicion of great wealth."[3]

Jim Harries elaborates on the source of the prosperity gospel in Africa, which Martin acknowledged is linked to the phenomenon in Latin America. He asserts, "Assisted by the 'magical' basis to African life, . . . African people have instead appropriated the 'prosperity gospel' as a means of understanding that God himself stands behind the 'whites.'"[4] In other words, Africans in general often assume that the prosperity of white people is attributable to powerful magic coming from their Christian God. They may then view Christianity as a gateway to their own prosperity and they may seek attachments to white people in order to share in their wealth.

The flipside to gaining wealth and power in Africa, however, is that this same prosperity can make one the target of witchcraft from those who are envious. So while "the positive side of the perpetuation of 'superstition' is 'prosperity gospel,' . . . [which] proclaims success in life for all who truly believe, . . . any lack of good results from the evil orientation of human hearts . . . [and] results in a search for a witch."[5] In Africa, the witch is "a person with an evil heart,"[6] and "people who believe in witchcraft . . . propagate jealousy, suspicion, distrust, and hatred within a community."[7]

Notably, Isaac did not espouse the prosperity gospel nor unduly attach himself to white people to accomplish his mission. Nevertheless, he was targeted by witchcraft as people assumed he possessed great magic or secret connections. Witchcraft was one source of Isaac's suffering. He once related to me that someone planted a horn in the ground with its tip pointing upwards in a narrow gateway that he would often walk through. The horn's tip was covered with traditional "medicine" designed in this case to make him sick or die if he should happen to step on it. As Jim Harries said, the reason for such an evil act lies in the pervasive witchcraft that feeds off of jealousy

2. Ibid., 76.
3. Ibid.
4. Harries, *Vulnerable Mission*, 71.
5. Ibid., 8.
6. Ibid.
7. Ibid., 211.

and suspicion. Traditional Tongas disliked Isaac's disregard for customs and suspected he had contact with whites that made him powerful. In fact, it was his deep conviction that Jesus would protect him from witchcraft that allowed him merely to dig up the horn and discard it as a powerless object.

Summary

Anyone who is a real disciple of Jesus will face suffering or persecution. How could it be otherwise when the one we follow died on the cross despite his innocence? Not only does a Christian countercultural lifestyle attract opposition from non-Christians, but also from what the Bible calls "the powers of this dark world" and "the spiritual forces of evil in the heavenly realms" (Eph 6:12). That is why Paul insists that every Christian will suffer persecution (2 Tim 3:12). He expected obstacles and suffering as part of his walk with God. But how does a disciple prepare to face opposition?

Paul understood that all spiritual attacks against Christian workers are ultimately the work of Satan and his demonic forces. Fellow humans may be used by Satan, but they are not the real source of opposition, because they can potentially be won to Christ, just as Paul was when he opposed Christianity. Paul asserted, "For our struggle is not against flesh and blood" (Eph 6:12). Africans tend to fear those assumed to have contact with spirits, as they instinctively understand that spiritual power is no match for mere human strength. But Christians can learn to face even the fiercest sorcerers in Jesus' name. Numbers 23:23 says, "There is no sorcery against Jacob, no divination against Israel." Africans who understand that can withstand all kinds of threats that cause others to cave in to fear. Those who successfully learn to wage spiritual warfare become capable of training other effective leaders.

6

Training Leaders

In Chapter 2, we saw how Isaac soaked up training for himself in preparation for taking the gospel back to his home. Now in the mode of 2 Timothy 2:2, he needed to train others. This verse says, "And the things you have heard me say in the presence of many witnesses entrust to reliable men who will also be qualified to teach others." Isaac instinctively sought out such people to train, not only so they could participate in his ministry, but also so they could take it over one day. Without a chain of disciples, any ministry will soon die out.

Someone once said that we need FAT people in order for a ministry to be productive long-term, where "F" stands for faithful, "A" stands for able, and "T" stands for teachable. "Faithful" matches the word "reliable" in the verse above, meaning the person has a track record of dependability, keeping promises and commitments. "Able" matches the word "qualified," meaning the person is capable of teaching others, has enough zeal and time to dedicate to that, and is gifted in guiding people in the right direction. "Teachable" means the person is not so arrogant as to think he or she knows everything; there is a strong desire to learn by listening to others. So Isaac was looking to duplicate himself in his own converts who showed these characteristics.

Because he focused on young people from the start, Isaac had a ready supply of potential leaders to train. Not having a good education himself, he seemed drawn to those youngsters who were getting educated, as they could eventually offer things to the body of Christ that he lacked. But we have noted that it was not smooth sailing, as young people also have minds of their own. In Isaac's case, as we saw, most of the young people were

Training Leaders

lured away from his leadership by others who were anxious to have their own successful ministries. Through steadiness, determination, and sheer tenacity, Isaac managed to get many of them back in time. There remained another obstacle, however: the generation gap between him and them.

No one can really duplicate himself or herself because no two people live identical lives, especially two people of different generations. Since everyone faces different experiences, each one will have at least a slightly different philosophy of what is important. And yet leaders need to reproduce themselves for their life's work to endure. That is why organizations and faiths evolve and change, because those who succeed the founders are not only in a different environment, but they also have different experiences and values. Christianity has certainly evolved, despite its core of essential beliefs and its documents that include the Bible.

Andrew Walls described the evolution of Christianity over the centuries in terms of a shift in its "center of gravity." Saying that "Christian expansion is serial,"[1] he explained, "The first change in the centre of gravity of the Christian world . . . took place within the first century of the Christian era."[2] This was the movement described in the Book of Acts from the starting point of Jerusalem at the heart of the Jewish faith into the Hellenistic world of the eastern Roman Empire. Soon Jerusalem was destroyed, but this did little to slow the expansion of Christianity because the center of gravity had already moved away from Palestine. As it migrated, the flavor of Christianity changed, settling into a "Hellenistic-Roman model."[3] The Hellenistic model within the Roman Empire represented only the epicenter, as other versions of Christianity expanded into Persia, India, and Africa at about the same time.[4]

But even the epicenter of Christianity soon moved beyond the Roman Empire, especially into so-called "barbarian" realms. "A new model of Christianity developed among the Celtic and Germanic peoples between the Atlantic and the Carpathians, and another took its most distinctive shape among the Slavic peoples."[5] Europe was becoming the center of gravity for Christianity, and later by extension, its colonies overseas. Walls reckoned that over 90 percent of all Christians lived in Europe or North

1. Walls, *Cross-Cultural Process*, 30.
2. Ibid.
3. Ibid., 31.
4. Jenkins, *Lost History of Christianity*.
5. Walls, *Cross-Cultural Process*, 31.

Who Needs a Missionary?

America by AD 1800, but "today, something like 60 percent of them live in Africa, Asia, Latin America, or the Pacific."[6]

With each advance of Christianity into a new part of the globe, the previous heartland sadly withered. Walls commented on the reshaping of Christianity in the twentieth century, saying that its decline in Europe was "the most considerable recession from the Christian faith to occur since the early expansion of Islam," but the rapid growth of the faith outside traditional Christendom was "the most substantial accession to the Christian faith for at least a millennium."[7] For example, he estimated that the number of Christians in Africa rose from ten million in 1900 to three hundred million at the time of writing.[8]

With the constant shifting of its center of gravity, Christianity was also evolving as it came into contact with diverse cultures and settled there. Extrapolating the work of Walls and other mission researchers, Philip Jenkins popularized the notion of the "global South" as the epicenter of Christianity, predicting that "Africa and Latin America would be in competition for the title of the most Christian continent" by 2025.[9] He emphasized, "As Christianity moves South, it is in some ways returning to its roots" as a non-Western religion."[10] Certainly the Western domination of Christianity for so long has placed a secular stamp on the faith which is unlikely to remain intact as the center moves out of the West. Jenkins stated, "The types of Christianity that have thrived most successfully in the global South have been very different from what many Europeans and North Americans consider mainstream."[11]

The kind of faith that Isaac possesses comes from Scripture as read through the lens of his traditional African worldview, as well as from influences he had while developing his own ministry. Jenkins describes Christianity in the global South as "far more enthusiastic, much more centrally concerned with the immediate workings of the supernatural."[12] This is not really surprising: Christianity always adapts to its surroundings, whether Jewish, Hellenistic, European, Slavic, Persian, Indian, or in the global

---

6. Ibid.
7. Ibid.
8. Ibid.
9. Jenkins, *Next Christendom*, 3.
10. Ibid., 15.
11. Ibid., 107.
12. Ibid.

South. In Africa, people are concerned with spiritual answers to everyday happenings, so it is normal when Christianity adopts these concerns too. Jenkins asserted that "Southern types of Christianity . . . have in almost all cases remained within very recognizable Christian traditions," preaching a "strong and even pristine Christian message."[13]

Jenkins may be overly optimistic about the orthodoxy of most Christianity in the global South. The episodes already mentioned where Isaac confronted other versions of Christianity in his home area show that some of these sects draw more from African traditions than historical Christianity. Not all accept the core doctrine that Jesus is Lord of all. From the beginning, as Christianity spread, there were unorthodox brands of the faith spawned as well. For example, the Arians arose in the early church in Alexandria, Egypt teaching that Jesus was a created being below the Father. As Christianity spread in the United States, two well-known faiths based on Christianity arose and remain unorthodox: Jehovah's Witnesses and Mormons. Jehovah's Witnesses are a newer version of the Arian heresy, while Mormons teach that everyone can become a god. In Africa, some branches of the *VaPostori* (Apostles) teach that their founder is the Messiah for Africa.

The *VaPostori* derive from Zimbabwean Shona prophets who arose in the 1930s in reaction to colonial oppression of Africans and to the European Christianity they encountered. They preached a hybrid religion, drawing from African traditions, the Old Testament, and from the prophet John the Baptist. Their evangelists and missionaries went all over southern and central Africa preaching repentance and baptism in order to enter a new way of life that remained totally African. Today the *VaPostori* are easily recognized by their men whose heads are shaved and beards full-grown, as well as their women dressed in white standing on street corners selling handmade items or exchanging currency. Their cross-border trading and hard work have made them into prosperous cults.

For a class taught by Paul Hiebert on Folk Religions that I took by correspondence from Fuller Theological Seminary, I investigated one *VaPostori* sect founded by Johane Masowe, a famous Shona prophet from eastern Zimbabwe.[14] Masowe adopted this name meaning "John of the Wilderness," indicating that he now represented John the Baptist after he had a

---

13. Ibid., 108.
14. Reese, "Johane Masowe."

religious experience in 1932.[15] He began preaching from that time until his death in 1973 that Africans needed to repent and be baptized, spreading the Masowe sect of *VaPostori* all over southern, central, and eastern Africa.

While there is some debate about whether Masowe thought of himself as a messianic figure, his followers certainly take him to be the Messiah for Africa.[16] In my investigations for Hiebert's class, I was required to attend a worship service of the group being studied. With the *VaPostori*, that was easier said than done. For three months I kept seeking permission from elders of the Bulawayo congregation to attend their Sabbath worship, but they kept putting me off. When I finally showed up two different Saturday mornings trying to join them in worship, they quickly cut me off, saying I had no permission to be there; clearly they are suspicious of white people. I had to leave both times and ask the elders for permission to attend their services once again. Finally, sensing my determination, they agreed to let me attend a one-hour session called the *Hosanna Mukuru*.

Held from 9:00 am to 10:00 am on Saturdays, the *Hosanna Mukuru* is the service described by Clive Dillon-Malone as consisting of singing the "Great Hosanna" at the beginning of the hour.[17] My assistant (there to help me understand Shona) and I entered a large hall completely void of furniture, with only one small photo of Johane Masowe on the front wall. Men sat at the front on the bare concrete floor, with women and children behind, all dressed in white and barefoot. An elder approached a door leading to a side room, squatting and clapping in the Shona attitude of respect, opened the door and then closed it. A minute later, nine women dressed in white entered the worship hall and took their place between the men and the women. These were the Sisters, some of whom never marry, as they are devoted to prayer.[18]

A worship leader then shouted, "*Imbai!*" ("Sing!") in Shona and everyone sang the word "Hosanna" repeatedly until the song melted into high-volume unison prayer, finally returning to singing, "Hosanna, Hallelujah!" for fifteen to twenty minutes altogether. Interspersed with the singing and prayers there was a sound of deep groaning and growling, which my assistant and I assumed to be coming from men who were designated prophets;

---

15. Dillon-Malone, *Korsten Basketmakers*, 12, 16.
16. Daneel, *Quest for Belonging*, 139, 180.
17. Dillon-Malone, *Korsten Basketmakers*, 75.
18. Ibid., 65–66.

the groaning would indicate the activity of the Spirit in them.[19] Finally, a preacher gave a sermon in Shona, which was translated into the local Ndebele. The sermon briefly recounted the history of the Masowe *VaPostori* from Adam to the present day. The preacher maintained that the gospel passed from Adam through the Israelite patriarchs up to Jesus, who was killed by the Jews. Then, he said, the gospel fell into obscurity until Johane Masowe recovered it in 1932. From the sermon, my assistant and I both got the strong impression that his followers take Masowe to be the Messiah for Africa.

The Masowe sect does not represent traditional Christianity, nor was it propagated by missionaries. It is rightly called a New Religious Movement (NRM) because it takes ingredients from various sources and amalgamates them into something different. NRMs appeal to local populations because they almost always promise a revitalization of an oppressed culture, a return to traditional values with some innovations, with a messianic figure who promises the start of a golden age under his leadership. Yet they also fail to deliver the promises of such a heady agenda and in the end they settle into a shell of dull orthodoxy. For example, the preacher at the Masowe church summed up the prophet's message as an admonition to shave the head and wear white, rather than the original message to repent and be baptized.

An almost invisible thread that ties all forms of Christianity together, besides the Good Shepherd who leads us and the Scriptures that guide us, is the communication of the faith that has always accompanied the movement of the center of gravity. The missionary movement in each case assisted in the survival of Christianity by reaching new heartlands with the gospel before the old ones collapsed. As Western missionaries preached, and people were converted, they were taught how to propagate and organize the faith. Walls suggested that the missionary movement "was for most of its life a peripheral and minority concern within Western Christianity."[20] Without that thin line of missionaries the faith could not advance; without the process of making disciples, Christianity could not be propagated.

While missionaries are indispensible to the spread of the gospel to new cultures, they are often only indirectly involved in the evolution of the faith in that new place. For example, I discovered a chain of churches in Mozambique that had been founded by indigenous evangelists converted

---

19. Ibid., 82–83.
20. Walls, *Cross-Cultural Process*, 33.

Who Needs a Missionary?

to Christ in refugee camps in Malawi, where they went to escape the Mozambican civil war. Malawian Christians converted by missionaries of the Church of Christ had taught the Mozambicans the gospel in the camps, and when they were repatriated they went all over northern Mozambique starting what they knew of the Church of Christ. They launched what is now called a Church Planting Movement (CPM), which is something like Roland Allen's concept of the "spontaneous expansion of the church."[21] Before any missionaries had arrived, indigenous evangelists had planted hundreds of churches spontaneously.

In 2001, my son and I accompanied a group on a two-week mission trip to Pebane on the Mozambican coast. We planned to show the Jesus film as often as we could during the two weeks and decided to cooperate with three evangelical churches in Pebane: the Assemblies of God, the Baptists, and the Church of Christ where we camped. It was my first time to experience this indigenous brand of the Church of Christ that turned out to be quite unlike the church I had grown up in. In one regard, it was similar: as soon as one of our mission team members brought out a guitar and began playing worship songs at our camp, the Church of Christ preacher immediately objected. No musical instruments were allowed to be played for worship on church property.

That caused most of our team to worship more with the Baptists, but I was fascinated with this Church of Christ and accepted an invitation to preach there one Sunday. While the American Church of Christ prides itself on congregational singing that sounds good without instruments, this Mozambican church's singing was awful to my ears. Being accustomed to hearty singing by Africans, I was quite surprised that the worship sounded more like a funeral service, with sad dirges as hymns. I didn't know enough of the local culture to know if this was indigenous or if it was brought in from Malawi, but I couldn't understand how Africans could sound so dreary in worship.

That Sunday one man came forward for baptism after my sermon. The local preacher surprised me by saying that since I had been the preacher when he came forward, I must do the counseling. So I asked the man what had made him decide to request baptism. He replied in typical African fashion that it was in response to a dream that he had travelled a long distance to attend this service and request baptism. The congregation prepared to walk to the nearest river, but I decided not to go, as I thought our mission

---

21. Allen, *Spontaneous Expansion of the Church*.

group might have to leave before they returned. In fact, they did return before we left, and the way they returned surprised me again. While they were a long way off, I could hear excited singing at high volume but didn't know where it was coming from. As they drew nearer, I realized that the same people who had been singing dirges a couple of hours before were now in full-throated excitement over the baptism. Neighborhoods all over Pebane must have known that someone had been baptized that day. As the church group arrived with the new convert in the church yard, they were absolutely exuberant, dancing and singing for all they were worth. They were Africans after all!

I didn't stay long enough in Pebane to get any real understanding of how this Church of Christ functioned, but it was clear that in the absence of missionaries it was different, not only from traditional Churches of Christ, but also from most other African churches. Missionaries have been trying to catch up with these indigenous churches to inject more familiar doctrines and values into their Christianity, but one wonders if they can ever totally succeed. Still these churches were not like the *VaPostori* in failing to keep central Christian doctrines.

Although it adapts to its surroundings, Christianity has amazingly held throughout the centuries a core of central teaching that tells most converts that groups like Jehovah's Witnesses, Mormons, or *VaPostori* are off the mark. Where they err is in their understanding of Jesus. Isaac kept Jesus as the center of his faith and prayers, whereas those other sects demote Jesus to a lesser being. The number one thing to be passed on to newer leaders is who Jesus is and the need to trust him for all ministry.

Among the Abrahamic faiths, only Christianity considers Jesus to be divine. That creates a stumbling block for Jews and Muslims as well as many others, who still cannot imagine that someone equal to God could die on a cross. The apostle Paul encountered that in the first century among Greeks and Jews: "For the message of the cross is foolishness to those who are perishing, but to us who are being saved it is the power of God. . . . Jews demand miraculous signs and Greeks look for wisdom, but we preach Christ crucified, a stumbling block to Jews and foolishness to Gentiles" (1 Cor 1:18, 22–23).

For both Muslims and Jews, the Trinity is counterintuitive to what they know about God. So how did Christianity come to the conclusion that Jesus is divine and that God exists within a Trinity? Muslims and Jews see the Trinity as belief in three gods, whereas Christians claim to be just as monotheistic as they are. Of course the Trinity is not a word you can find in the Bible, but the concept is definitely there. We first see the Trinity at Jesus' baptism. In Matthew 3:16–17, it says that as soon as Jesus was baptized, heaven opened and the Spirit of God descended like a dove and lighted on him, while a voice from heaven said, "This is my Son, whom I love; with him I am well pleased."

The Trinity was something of a *fait accompli* at that point, even if people did not understand the concept. Those who encountered Jesus always had to make up their minds about who he was, and those who followed him came to see him as Son of God (Matt 16:16; John 1:49). They came to call him Lord, a title usually reserved by Jews for God alone (Rom 10:9–12; Rev 19:16). When they called Jesus Lord and king, early Christians were taken to mean that they owed him more loyalty than they owed to Caesar (Acts 17:7). Lest there be any doubt how they felt about Jesus, Thomas called him "my Lord and my God" (John 20:28), and Paul said he was equal to God and that every knee would bow to him one day (Phil 2:6, 10).

The issue of worship in the early church makes it clear that the first Christians took Jesus to be divine. Larry Hurtado did a study of New Testament worship and concluded, "In the earliest observable stages of Christian worship in the New Testament, devotion is offered to God the Father and to (and through) Jesus."[22] For example, John saw no problem with the worship of the Lamb in heaven as well as worship of God on the throne (Rev 5:13), yet worship of angels was unacceptable (Rev 19:10; 22:8–9). While this was trinitarian worship, Hurtado emphasizes that in practice it was more "binitarian," since Christians have usually offered more worship to Jesus and God than to the Holy Spirit.[23]

Despite the persistent worship of Jesus for twenty centuries, Hurtado makes it clear that from the beginning, Christians did not see this as contradicting the unity of God. Obviously this was something new added on to Jewish concepts of acceptable worship. Hurtado explains that "Christ is included with God as a recipient of devotion that can properly be understood as worship."[24] The connection between God the Father, God the Son, and God the Holy Spirit is, in other words, so close that there remains only a single God. And there is no other god, spirit, or angel worthy of worship.

---

22. Hurtado, *Origins of Christian Worship*, 63.
23. Ibid., 64.
24. Ibid., 71–72.

Without the Jesus phenomenon, there would be no Trinity, so the worship of Jesus simply came out of trying to make sense of who Jesus is. Christians concluded that there was no option but to take him to be Savior, Lord, and God within the monotheism of Judaism. Hurtado insists that Christians did not just take liberties to make these drastic changes to Judaism, but "they felt required to do so by God."[25] He adds, "Had these Christians not been anxious to be monotheists, their life would have been much simpler!"[26]

That is also pretty much the way Isaac understands the Trinity. He experienced Jesus as equal to God right from the beginning, praying to him, worshipping him, and seeing him work in his ministry. It doesn't take a trained theologian to get the Trinity, just a believer in the life, death, and resurrection of Jesus who seeks his intervention in ministry. As a practitioner rather than a theologian, Isaac passes on to his own disciples what he has experienced by letting them watch him in action. Training is a hands-on activity.

Robert Coleman described Jesus' training methods in his short book *The Master Plan of Evangelism*. Noting that Jesus would not be called a successful evangelist by today's standards, because he had so few visible disciples when his ministry ended,[27] Coleman insists that Jesus concentrated on training a few reliable people to continue his ministry after he was gone. Thus the training actually became more important than evangelism, even though it could not be done in isolation from evangelism.

Jesus selected relatively few uneducated men for training. Coleman says, "One cannot transform the world except as individuals in the world are transformed."[28] He selected these few "that they might be with him and that he might send them out to preach and to have authority to drive out demons" (Mark 3:14–15). In other words, the training came from intimate association with Jesus and his ministry to the masses. The disciples had to be ready to follow him wherever he led and to do what he said. This process provided a means of winnowing out those who merely said they would like to follow from those who meant it.

We began to follow this pattern in our ministry in Zimbabwe, providing opportunities for young people to test their commitment and gifting

---

25. Ibid., 97.
26. Ibid., 105.
27. Coleman, *Master Plan of Evangelism*, 28.
28. Ibid., 23–24.

for ministry. One young man, a convert from a farm church in Esigodini, asked if we would fund his bid to study at a Bible school in Harare. As he was in his late teens, we urged him instead to enter our apprentice program to test his desire to serve God in fulltime ministry. This proved to be a smart plan; after six months of apprenticeship he resigned, saying ministry was simply too difficult for him! He opted instead to become a policeman, and we certainly need Christian police. We grew in our conviction that fulltime Bible studies should be reserved for those who had already proved they could conduct successful ministries.

None of Isaac's disciples has so far had fulltime Bible studies; that could have ruined what God was doing through Isaac's hands-on training with his select few. They are learning where it counts, in the rough and tumble of ordinary ministry alongside Isaac. In return, Isaac gives of himself to his disciples, as Jesus did. In Isaac's case, he has to show his followers how to balance the needs of a hungry family with the needs of ministry in a place where there are no fulltime ministers. In Jesus' case, he could impart far more: the intimate knowledge of God walking among them, showing his compassion for the lost and needy.

Coleman lists a four-step process in training disciples once they have been selected and prove dedicated. He calls the steps "demonstration," "delegation," "supervision," and "reproduction."[29] Briefly, demonstration meant that Jesus "saw to it that his disciples learned his way of living with God and man."[30] The followers watched Jesus' lifestyle, including his prayer life and his ministry. They heard him teach and saw him heal and drive out demons. They saw his closeness to the Father and his knowledge of Scripture. They witnessed his compassion. Coleman says, "His training classes were never dismissed."[31]

Once they had seen the pattern of his ministry, he delegated ministry to them bit by bit. "Jesus was always building his ministry for the time when his disciples would have to take over his work."[32] Starting with the delegation of small things, like arranging for food or places to stay, Jesus eventually sent out disciples on specific short missions without him (Matt 10:1; Luke 10:1). His advice for these missions still applies: "Whatever town or village you enter, search for some worthy person there and stay at his house

29. Ibid., 63–97.
30. Ibid., 63.
31. Ibid., 68.
32. Ibid., 71.

Training Leaders

until you leave" (Matt 10:11). Although they might experience rejection, persecution, and hardship, they would look for responsive people to preach to and lead them to watch for the approaching kingdom of God. The home of a "man of peace" (Luke 10:6) might end up becoming a house church later on.

Once they returned from these limited missions, the disciples would report back to Jesus for what we would call a debriefing, but which Coleman calls "supervision."[33] Success or failure was not the focus; Jesus wanted the disciples to focus on what God was doing in bringing in his kingdom. He said, "I saw Satan fall like lightning from heaven" (Luke 10:18), and "Do not rejoice that spirits submit to you, but rejoice that your names are written in heaven" (Luke 10:20). The disciples were part of a much larger mission directed from heaven itself, but for now they sorely needed guidance and encouragement. While he was still with them in the flesh, Jesus never lost an opportunity to review what had happened in the daily ministry, asking questions and drawing out lessons that would be remembered in the final phase when he ascended back to heaven.

Coleman calls the fourth and final stage of discipleship training "reproduction." By this he meant that Jesus' "ministry in the Spirit would be duplicated manyfold by his ministry in the lives of his disciples."[34] Amazingly, Jesus had no other plan than that his few disciples should reproduce his ministry after his ascension.[35] Among his last words to the disciples before his death, resurrection, and departure, Jesus told them, "This is to my Father's glory, that you bear much fruit, showing yourselves to be my disciples" (John 15:8). Without a perpetual chain of disciples making other disciples, Jesus' plan of evangelism would have failed. Ministry must be reproduced in each generation and that takes training.

Coleman's four stages of discipleship training correspond fairly closely to what Paul Hersey and Kenneth Blanchard call the four modes of "situational leadership" whereby leaders change their leadership style depending on the readiness of followers.[36] In the term "readiness," Hersey and Blanchard include both ability and willingness to perform tasks.[37] That is, followers may start out without much experience or skill and thus may also

---

33. Ibid., 81.
34. Ibid., 89.
35. Ibid., 91.
36. Hersey and Blanchard, *Management of Organizational Behavior*, 170.
37. Ibid., 175.

be reluctant to perform a task set by the leader. When readiness is low, the leader needs to provide maximum guidance with specific instructions and close supervision, demonstrating how to do the task. Hersey and Blanchard call this "telling" because it is high on task and low on discussion.[38]

In the second stage, the followers are still inexperienced but are trying hard to learn how to do the task. While willingness is high, ability is still low. Now the leadership style becomes more interactive, encouraging the followers' efforts; at the same time, the leader's directive style is still high because of the followers' inexperience. Hersey and Blanchard call this "selling" because it is motivational and promotes greater understanding of what the task is all about.[39]

In the third stage, the followers are gaining experience but still lack confidence to do the task alone. Now the leader becomes more motivational and supportive but less directive. The followers now possess the skills and understanding that go with the task, but need to grow in confidence. Hersey and Blanchard call this "participating" because the leader works with the followers as a team.[40]

In the final stage, the followers are fully capable of performing the task on their own. They have both ability and willingness to do the task, so the leader may disengage while maintaining overall supervision. Hersey and Blanchard call this "delegating" because the leader allows the followers to take over the task.[41]

Going back to Isaac, he was not as analytical as Hersey and Blanchard. Nor did he analyze the methods of Jesus' discipleship training as Robert Coleman did. But he had gone through a little systematic training himself and he made sure his own disciples did some training also. What we saw was the end product rather than the process. We arrived in 2003 with a team from the United States to do some events for Isaac's churches. We had a good team prepared to do children's ministry as well as leadership training over a weekend. These events took place during daylight hours, as there is no electricity in Magobbo. During the evenings there were regular church services held by the light of a couple of kerosene lamps. The church building by this time had an asbestos roof held up by steel pillars; there

---

38. Ibid., 171.
39. Ibid., 178.
40. Ibid., 178–79.
41. Ibid., 179.

were no walls, which wasn't bad in the hot climate. So the light of the moon and stars was visible from under the roof.

Villagers from the vicinity arrived and camped out during our stay so as to be involved in all events. Some had walked from as far as ten miles away, while those who lived closer could go home to sleep. All of the churches Isaac planted were represented. Makeshift reed enclosures were quickly erected to provide areas for cooking, sleeping, and bathing. There was a festive atmosphere as the Tongas love visitors and big events.

As soon as we arrived, we introduced Isaac to our team and informed him of our plans for our time with him. Many of those who host our teams from overseas allow the Americans to do what they want without comment, so as to please the visitors. Isaac, however, had a different proposal. He said, "You may preach, but we also want to preach each evening." He wanted his trainees to have a chance to preach in front of us and he proceeded to give them twice as many opportunities that weekend as we had. That is unusual for such events where most Africans, used to the colonial system, let the visiting white folks take charge.

Isaac had about fifteen men he was training, most of them much younger than himself. When they preached, it was evident they knew the Scripture and had a firm grasp of their theology. Thus it proved to be a blessing to us that Isaac insisted on letting them do the bulk of the preaching while we were there. It let us know for certain that his churches are "Four Self" churches. That is, they had learned to do theology for themselves, so are self-theologizing. That is the real goal of training disciples, so they can think for themselves using the Bible, prayer, and communal discussion as their guide.

Summary

Paul systematically set about training younger men as disciples, so that he never served alone in ministry. He took these men with him on his travels and gave them assignments to carry out in his absence, just as Jesus had done earlier with his selected apostles. Such chains of discipleship are what have helped the Christian faith to survive down to our time, passing on God's truth and Christian practice from generation to generation. Ministry should always outlast one person, and preparation must be made for others to pick up the banner of service and to live for Christ.

Who Needs a Missionary?

While many models of discipleship have been used through the ages, the one that Isaac used was first learned by his assistant, Francis Mudimba, in Bulawayo. Because of his educational level, Francis could take courses available in English, whereas Isaac could not. Towards the end of our time in Zimbabwe, we were introduced to a basic curriculum of discipleship known as Bible Training Centre for Pastors (BTCP). Once again, Agrippa Dube spearheaded that endeavor to equip pastoral leaders with basic teaching and literature. Since the curriculum was devised in the USA, it is book-centered and classroom-based, which suited Francis more than Isaac. BTCP covers ten topics: Hermeneutics, Bible Survey, Bible Doctrines, Spiritual Life, Church Ministry, Church History, Preaching, Teaching, Evangelism, and Missions. Francis devoured these classes and then, as the program is reproducible, began to train others. It was these Tonga trainees whom we encountered as such developed disciples at Magobbo. When Francis died an early death, the training program was hit hard. Enough people had been trained, however, that Christian discipleship began to impact the community, even the non-Christians.

7

Transforming the Community

Although I was born in Zimbabwe, I went through elementary school in a small rural community in Arkansas. I feel pretty sure that that community was transformed by the gospel when frontier evangelists fresh from the Second Great Awakening arrived in the vicinity to preach. But that would have happened a century or so before my birth, so all I saw was the long-term result. My experience included regular "gospel meetings" on summer evenings when fired-up evangelists once again unleashed severe warnings and sweet promises of pardon to packed churches. It was during one such event that I went forward to be baptized because of my sins; I was eleven years old.

Maybe it was just my own family, but it seemed that life in Ravenden Springs, Arkansas revolved around church and family. Almost all my relatives belonged to the same small church; everyone else who lived in the village seemed to be a member of one of the three churches there. But like the summer evangelists, I knew that there remained some unrepentant sinners in the community. I remember when we were warned as schoolchildren not to walk around the town center one day because a noted rabble-rouser had made a trip all the way to the Missouri line to get liquored up and was soon expected to roar down the only street in town in a drunken state without regard for human life. We were generally very safe in Ravenden Springs, partly because the mischief makers could not even buy alcohol in our "dry" county.

The teachers at our public school were mostly all connected to a church, so that our lives in public and private were virtually the same, or so it seemed to me as a boy. Christian principles seemed to pervade the atmosphere and any deviation was punished. It probably helped that the community was homogeneous with few outsiders and only one ethnic group: Scotch-Irish, and all of them from conservative Protestant roots. The most unchurch-like memory I have of my childhood is being taught square-dancing by one of the younger teachers who had lived in a distant place and was considered innovative.

There were no pool halls—or other dens of ill repute—in town. One farming family operated a dance floor in a barn near town, but only people considered lukewarm Christians, or outside the gospel, frequented such a place. Movies were shown in an unused general store, but the "picture shows" were all "G" rated, such as the adventures of Hopalong Cassidy, a favorite cowboy of the time. There were few places where a boy could get in serious trouble. We didn't even own a car; the downtown consisted of a row of stores that was one block long, and we could easily walk wherever we needed to go in town.

But we grew up in Ravenden Springs not really knowing what the village was like before the gospel arrived in power. No one alive could remember that far back. Looking back now, I realize that lots of small churches must have been planted within a short time, since they still dot the countryside, and that their planting must have introduced major changes into the life of the community. But now I imagine it to be something like when Isaac arrived with the gospel for the first time in Magobbo; that is where I have witnessed both the before and after of the transformation brought by Christianity.

Let me confess here that I never expected to see any overall transformation of the community around Magobbo. First of all, as I have just said, I was not familiar with such a change as I had never experienced it from start to finish. Second, I remain something of a Western skeptic, who consistently underestimates what the gospel can do among remote Africans. Third, I did not consider community transformation as a logical or even necessary consequence of gospel preaching although I knew it was theoretically possible. But now I have seen it with my own eyes, yet I cannot really explain it. So if you are looking in these pages for a how-to guide for such transformation, you will probably be disappointed, as all I can say is that it happened because of the gospel itself.

Transforming the Community

Magobbo in 1987

What was Magobbo like when Isaac returned to preach the gospel in 1987? I have reported on that somewhat in earlier chapters, but it would help to give a summary of what I witnessed during my first visits. I cannot think of any more remote place in Zimbabwe than Magobbo, even though I visited hidden corners of the country during my childhood during school holidays while I was in high school in the 1960s. My father worked for the government department of National Parks and Wildlife, beginning as a humble game ranger in some of the wildest places in the country: Kariba Town near the Kariba Dam as it was nearing completion on the Zambezi River, Chipinda Pools in the Gonarezhou National Park, and Marongora in the Mana Pools National Park. During school breaks, my brother John and I would travel to these places to stay a few weeks. We enjoyed the wild remoteness and sometimes traveled with Dad into tribal areas where chiefs or headmen had called for assistance with troublesome wild animals.

But none of those places seems as remote as Magobbo. The tar road ends at Binga town on Lake Kariba and there follows a bone-jarring ride over eighty kilometers of dirt road to reach Nagangala near Siabuwa. From there it is another seven kilometers down trails made for scotch-carts, heading toward the mountains that form the boundary of Chizarira National Park. Every time I visit Magobbo, I feel that I have entered a rare part of Zimbabwe where time has stood still. Isaac was able to build his home and till his fields without all the permission he would have needed elsewhere from chiefs and headmen. The land seemed so plentiful and open that there were few rules, except that one had to be Tonga to benefit. "Benefit" might seem too strong a word, as wild animals from the park would stream down from the hills during the harvest, and a pitched battle would ensue between man and beast for the privilege of eating the crops. Tsetse flies prevented the customary herding of livestock until the fly was eradicated.

Culture and customs seemed archaic in that part of Zimbabwe: women still had their upper front teeth knocked out and men still walked along carrying their trademark axes over their shoulders. The homemade axes functioned as a sign of Tonga masculinity and as protection against wild animals. Women smoked the peculiar gourd pipes that fit neatly into their mouths where the two front teeth were missing. Even fellow Zimbabweans who traveled with us to visit the Tongas felt some culture shock because of these practices that were unfamiliar to them.

Who Needs a Missionary?

Isaac points to a woman smoking a gourd pipe.

The resident *inyanga*, such as Isaac's maternal uncle, was the dominant spiritual figure in the rural communities. People consulted him (or her) for illness, misfortune, or curses (those received or those they wished to send). Isaac set up his own home right in the middle of his uncle's village at first just as any respectful Tonga nephew might do. So when we visited we also used to stay in the *inyanga*'s village, although at the time I was unaware of his actual status. On one visit, I did notice an animal horn filled with some type of *muthi*, which I was told was an antidote for snake bite. Spiritualism, as I have made clear in earlier chapters, was the predominant religion, holding people in real bondage to fear of forces over which they had no control.

Of all the villages I visited as a missionary, Magobbo had the greatest feeling of being right "in the bush," where it was easy to get away from humanity by simply walking off into the wilderness. While I have said earlier that time seemed to stand still there, that was only an impression not based on fact. If I had arrived a few decades earlier, there would have been no villages there at all, since the Tongas lived near the Zambezi until Kariba Dam was built. Also, it is not as if there were no public schools or churches in the area, but Magobbo itself had neither before Isaac began his ministry. Children who lived in Magobbo walked the seven kilometers to the main road at Nagangala for school each day and then back home at day's end, a huge undertaking for first graders! The nearest clinic was in Siabuwa, called a "growth point" in the jargon of Zimbabwe's rural development. The term simply meant that Siabuwa had several shops, including liquor stores, and a clinic, but it did not mean there was electricity. Siabuwa is about fifteen kilometers from Magobbo.

The only indication of government presence that I saw on my first trip to Magobbo was a solitary borehole, a hand-pumped well that spewed out water almost too salty to drink, no doubt because of the high salt content deep underground. I tasted it and afterwards generally brought and drank my own water. There was also a river that was dry most of the year, like most rivers in Zimbabwe. Water could be found in the sandy river bed, however, by digging. Part of the daily drill in the early morning was to send the women and girls off to the water source with buckets on their heads, while the men and boys milked the cows and goats, and then led them off to find pasture. It was a lifestyle that has changed very little for hundreds of years all over Africa.

Needless to say, the mortality rate was high, as health care was minimal and tropical diseases were plentiful. Diseases like malaria were rampant and by 1987 AIDS had begun to take a toll on what few public health facilities existed. Life expectancy plummeted as AIDS proliferated, with no effective treatment available at that time. As we have seen, Isaac lost some of those nearest and dearest to him through various illnesses while they were still in early adulthood: his daughter Nomsa, his cousin and early convert Mpendulo, and his favorite disciple Francis. His wife, Margaret, suffered several serious bouts of malaria when she first moved to the Zambezi valley, and even now she has chronic asthma. Isaac has defied the odds by reaching his sixties still in good health, in a land where most men are dead within fifty years of their birth.

Magobbo in 2010

The last time I visited the Magobbo area was in 2010 when I spent a week at Kalonga doing a leadership training school for Isaac's church leaders. It was part of my annual trip to Zimbabwe, which I have taken since 2002 to do Bible schools for the churches we helped establish. Isaac usually brought leaders to Bulawayo for the school, and this year was no exception. However, I had promised him that eventually we would also hold a similar school for his leaders who couldn't come to the event in Bulawayo. Isaac had been mentoring numerous leaders, but only managed to bring a select group into the city for training. Now we had the opportunity to engage with all his leaders in their own setting.

We would do all teaching in the vernacular languages, and some of his advanced leaders would join me in teaching. I used Ndebele, since I have not learned Tonga; most Tonga men know Ndebele fluently, since it is taught in public schools from the earliest grades as a national language that is predominant in Matabeleland North, where the Binga District lies. For any who might not know Ndebele we had translation.

I got a teenager to drive me to Magobbo in a Ford Ranger pickup. He was a white Zimbabwean and familiar with the bush, as he had often taken Americans on short-term mission trips into rural areas of several neighboring countries. He packed two small tents, one for me and one for himself, as well as African-type food we would simply contribute to the common pot, as we would eat whatever our hosts ate. He brought bread, eggs, and tea for breakfast, and corn meal and cooking oil to contribute to other meals. Like most southern Africans, the Tongas prefer *isitshwala* as the staple diet; it is cornmeal porridge so thick that you eat it with your hands, dipping it in sauces to add some flavor.

Since we weren't able to contribute much to the sauces, we let our hosts provide the goats and vegetables that we ate as a group. The first day of the Bible school, someone dragged a protesting young goat by its leg into the campground and tied it to a tree. While we were in the middle of a lesson, suddenly several men jumped up and tore off to retrieve the goat that had managed to escape. Shortly they came dragging it back still protesting all the way to the cooking pot. We had arrived at a good time, as food was plentiful from the recent harvest.

Kalonga was a new place for me; I had often heard about it and knew the local church leaders quite well, as they always attended training sessions elsewhere, even those held in Bulawayo. The man I knew best, Jaison Tshuma, had lived in the city for some years, working with a local church there, and he now provided good leadership at Kalonga. Kalonga was only about five or six kilometers from Magobbo, and it definitely reflected Isaac's influence, since he helped plant the church there quite early on in his ministry. The village is located right at the base of a hill topped by a steep cliff, and that is where my driver spent his days hiking around the hillside with some local herd boys while I taught or listened to others teach down below.

Isaac climbing into an granary elevated to keep out pests.

As soon as we arrived, we backed the pickup into a small clearing where we could put up both tents. We were on the edge of a large clearing that contained both a primary school and a church building, plus the outhouses that served both institutions. The Tongas had constructed a thatch shelter for the Bible school so we could sit in the shade; even in mid-winter (July) the midday sun in Binga District got quite hot, but nights were refreshingly cool. Near the shelter were a couple of enclosures surrounded by reed walls; these were used both for sleeping quarters for those who had walked too far to return home at night and for daytime cooking.

Right behind our tents were some Tonga homes, one of them belonging to Phambanisa Mutale, another church leader. Phambanisa invited us over for our first meal, since the Bible school would not start till the next morning. I noticed how many fruit trees were in his yard: papayas, guavas, lemons, and grapefruit, many of them laden with fruit. He served a meal of the usual *isitshwala*, made from homegrown corn, and the sauce was made from okra that he got from his garden. Boiled okra becomes just a mass of green slime, very difficult to eat with your hands, but it is delicious with *isitshwala*.

Later, Phambanisa took us over to have a look at his garden. He had chosen a wet spot for its location, in a wide vlei that would stay moist underground even in the dry season. In the middle of the garden he had dug down to find water that he used to water the plants by hand. In fact it later became clear that he would get up at 3:00 am, when the moon was out, to water the whole garden so he wouldn't miss a day at the Bible school! And it was an extensive garden, a couple of acres full of a wide variety of both vegetables and fruit trees. I was beginning to see something of the transformation of the community, but I didn't know it yet.

As we made a brief tour of some of the neighboring homes, I saw how Christians were improving the diet of the whole community by donating fruit trees to almost everyone. As we visited homes of both Christians and non-Christians, Jaison and Phambanisa would explain that they had given their neighbors baby papaya trees or lemon trees for transplanting; now mature trees were laden with fruit for the whole community to enjoy right in their own yards. Tonga homes are what we might call villages, because they house several generations in numerous dwellings, some made of proper bricks, but most made of dried mud spread over a pole framework. The project to hand out fruit trees benefited a wide range of inhabitants of the Kalonga area.

But that was just the beginning. Phambanisa's garden was something of a model as well. He provided liberally of his produce during the Bible school, so that we ate a variety of healthy food as sauces for the *isitshwala*. Some had walked from communities up to twenty kilometers away and they could all see the abundance of this particular garden as well as taste its fruits. Phambanisa would regularly supply bunches of lemon for those who liked the juice squeezed into their hot tea in the mornings. That is a common way to ward off colds or to relieve them, as the winter usually brought epidemics of sniffles or even influenza.

Phambanisa's innovative gardening was all the more impressive because it was unusual. I remember hearing high praise of a late Christian in Zambia, Kambole Mpatamatenga, not only because of his faithfulness to the Lord in his non-Christian community, but also because he was one of the few Tongas who showed initiative in seeking to improve village conditions, mostly through his hard work in developing a productive farm and cultivating fruit trees. He was a friend of my colleague, Allen Avery, and Allen tried hard to get other Tongas in southern Zambia to replicate Kambole's vision. However, he usually bemoaned the fact that few had Kambole's drive to water the young trees regularly when they needed it.

Transforming the Community

This commentary shows that although most Africans are successful farmers and have been for generations, they are not often innovative. Certainly farming techniques have improved and agricultural extension officers are now widely available, but Africans are quite often slow to make the recommended changes. For example, agricultural experts tell Africans in drought-prone areas such as Matabeleland not to grow so much maize, but they continue to do it anyway because of their hunger for *isitshwala*. While sorghum grows better in arid regions, it takes more work to thresh than maize. The increasing numbers of diabetics in southern Africa don't usually want to switch from *isitshwala* to sorghum as their staple diet, even though sorghum is much healthier for them.

As successful as Kambole was in developing a model farm and growing a variety of fruit trees, he was not as successful in spreading these innovations to his neighbors. Even though what the Kalonga Christians were doing in promoting the ubiquity of fruit trees in the area does not sound like much, it was actually village transformation. Furthermore, it is likely that such innovation could only come from a changed worldview. A large part of the reason that Africans may not wish to change ancient farming methods has to do with their cultural perspective, in particular their belief in witchcraft.

Back in Chapter 4, we told the story of Jim Harries going to Zambia as an agricultural missionary, only to find that local farmers did not want his easy solutions to their problems with hunger. The reason was that if one farmer, like a Kambole or a Phambanisa, began to outshine others, he would become both the target for requests for handouts and also, more ominously, the target for witchcraft. When one person stands out from the crowd, it is perceived as inappropriate and may create enough jealousy that enemies try to bring him or her down permanently through curses sent via specialist practitioners. The fact that Isaac's followers had not been brought down and continued to gain respect in the community was a sign of their tenacity and faith in God.

Farming in Binga District had become easier since 1987, when Tongas spent much time in their fields fending off wild animals from the ripening crops. By 2010, increased poaching had reduced the animal population of Chizarira National Park so antelopes, buffalos, and elephants were no longer much of a threat to the Tongas' food supply. Organized poachers from Zambia or from within the Zimbabwean government itself had begun to decimate the wildlife in protected parks. General lawlessness in Zimbabwe

Who Needs a Missionary?

has contributed to a growing tragedy for the nation's wildlife heritage, but this has made life easier for the Tongas.

In the brisk early morning air at Kalonga, as we were drinking our first cups of steaming tea while preparing for the day's Bible school, little children were already making their way to the village school right across the clearing from us. I was amazed to hear that this school was started by the church planted by Isaac, hence the church building was located in the same clearing. In fact, some classes were held in the church. The school was only for the lowest grades, from kindergarten to third grade. The tiny students would line up along the rows of stones painted white on the ground for morning assembly. The teachers would gather in front of the waiting pupils at around 7:30 am for the start of the school day. Almost all the teachers were young men who were Isaac's disciples, so it appeared the school was essentially a Christian school. This was confirmed when, after the singing of Zimbabwe's national anthem, the children marched off to their various classrooms singing, "We are marching in the light of God" in both English and Tonga.

Since we are used to the separation of church and state in the United States, it always surprises Americans when they discover that it is possible to teach the Bible in public schools in places like Zimbabwe. Some headmasters even invite visitors to preach to the entire assembly or to pray for them. This is not to say that all these administrators are Christians, but that they see no basic conflict between a religious and a secular education. And the school at Kalonga was both a Christian and a public school at the same time! I soon discovered that government education officers, in their desire to see satellite elementary schools in the area, invited Isaac's churches to develop schools for lower grades, using their own teachers and buildings while teaching the government curriculum. So not only was there now an official school at Kalonga, but one at Magobbo as well, sparing scores of youngsters from having to hike long distances in their early grades.

But what about the teachers? While it could not be guaranteed that all teachers would be Christians, Isaac had enough young converts who had completed their high school studies successfully that he could staff these two schools mostly with his own disciples. Public elementary school teaching in Binga District required only a high school education. You may recall that Isaac was a first grade dropout, but he valued education highly, sending all his own children to Nagangala Primary School despite the long distance they had to walk even when very small. He also surrounded himself in

Transforming the Community

ministry with smart youngsters, who outshone him in their education; that was not a threat to him but a way of complementing his own strengths with theirs. Francis Mudimba, it will be remembered, completed advanced level studies in Hwange and went on to become an excellent school teacher and church leader until his untimely death. Francis and Isaac made a formidable team despite the generation gap. Now Francis's younger brother was teaching at Kalonga Primary School.

Another sign of Isaac's impact on the larger community was in evidence at the Bible school itself. Some public officials were in attendance, confirming the stamp of approval that had been given to Christian influence over the government's education system. And all this in a supposedly Marxist state! Local government leaders urged Isaac and his leaders to keep up the good work of bringing quality education to little ones. They asked them to build permanent structures for the classrooms. It almost seemed to be an admission on the part of government that it was bankrupt and unable to provide the services that they now asked churches to provide. I wondered if they would permit the church building to remain as part of the campus.

The other major sign of Isaac's influence was that people attended the Bible school from various denominations. As stated in earlier chapters, Isaac was always careful not to steal sheep from other churches, even if they might try to steal his! He was basically starting up new churches where none already existed and then he insisted on working with neighboring churches from various backgrounds. This policy earned him great respect as a "clergyman" despite the fact that he was uneducated by most denominational standards. Now if he invited other churches to special events like the Bible school, some came. That never happened much in Ravenden Springs, Arkansas, as the three churches in town seemed to maintain separate spheres of influence, only mingling at funerals, as far as I can remember. So I was witnessing a transformation that extended to all Christians in the vicinity who were willing to cooperate.

Isaac was known as a cooperative man. He made himself available for various community projects. Back when wildlife prowled close to the Tonga huts at Magobbo, he became known as an expert tracker. National Parks would call in professional hunters to bring their foreign clients to hunt problem animals that encroached on Tonga fields, and one hunter always came first to Isaac's home to seek his help in finding the animals. Isaac formed a good team with the hunters, and the reward was usually lots of fresh meat, as the client hunters sought only trophies they could ship back to their homes.

In later years, Isaac teamed up with a white doctor based at Siabuwa. This doctor also happened to be an ardent follower of Jesus, so she and Isaac made another formidable team, as he helped her to gain access to communities to give inoculations to children and others susceptible to various diseases. This way, health care improved and it was all done in the name of Christ! For as long as the doctor remained in the area, she was certainly a valuable resource for the general community, helping it in its transformation due to the gospel.

Behind his cooperative spirit, I realized that Isaac has an entrepreneurial attitude that allows him to think outside the box in all these areas. In Chapter 4, I described how Isaac showed versatility in making a living. He tried many different options until he settled on growing just enough cotton to earn some annual cash, but for his regular income he was trying to launch a welding business in Siabuwa in 2010. This idea was truly innovative because Isaac would have a virtual monopoly on welding in a town that had no electricity. Maintaining the business would be difficult because someone would have to carry diesel from Binga township, eighty kilometers away, to fuel the generator. Welding rods would probably have to be bought in distant towns like Bulawayo. But these obstacles also ensured he would have no competition for the foreseeable future. He made this a family project involving his own sons, so they could grow in business experience with him.

The same entrepreneurial spirit was evident in the way Isaac approached his church work. He was willing to try numerous methods and work with different people for the sake of God's work. Sometimes he got burned for trusting people who were not trustworthy, but usually he was able to forge alliances that helped build God's kingdom, while contributing also to the transformation of the community. He built the same kind of entrepreneurial talent into those who became his disciples, at least as much as he could. This ensured a succession of new talent to further the cause of Christ in the area.

Personally, I don't think Isaac had community transformation as a specific goal, but it seemed to come naturally as an outgrowth of his deep faith in Jesus. He simply built a community of faith around him and had room for as many others as were willing to join him. He has deep convictions about standards for God's people and expects his own culture to change as a result of God's words and commands.

Of course he still has many neighbors who are not Christians, and they cannot be expected to accept his standards, but change in the vicinity is visible nonetheless. In addition to the elementary schools, gardens, and fruit trees, for example, I did not see any woman smoking a pipe in 2010, while I had encountered numerous older ladies doing that in 1987. On the other hand, I still heard the drums beating at night as I lay in my little tent, the sound carrying a long way in the cool night air; drums probably meant that someone had brewed beer and they were inviting the neighbors to join in an all-night drinking binge, probably in connection with ancestor worship. So more transformation is still needed.

What is the Kingdom of God?

When I was growing up in Ravenden Springs, Arkansas and in Harare, Zimbabwe I learned that the kingdom of God is the same as the church and sometimes I still hear that definition today. The phrase "kingdom of God" or "kingdom of heaven" occurs frequently in the gospels (about eighty-eight times by my own count). Matthew, written primarily for Jewish Christian readers originally, preferred "kingdom of heaven" because Jews were not allowed to pronounce the name of God, but the two phrases apparently mean the same thing. "Kingdom of heaven" first appears as the message preached by John the Baptist in Matthew 3:2, "Repent, for the kingdom of heaven is near." In my church, we read that as a prediction of the impending establishment of the church on the Day of Pentecost, but that is probably not what John meant.

Numerous hints of the kingdom come thick and fast in Matthew's gospel from its opening chapter. Matthew begins with a genealogy of Jesus that features King David prominently; he notes that Joseph, the earthly guardian of Jesus, was himself a son of David (Matt 1:20). Thus Jesus is firmly linked to the lineage of David, who established Israel's kingdom, which was seen as a model of God's kingdom on earth. The kingdom of Israel has never appeared more glorious than it did under David and Solomon. Palestinian Jews of Jesus' day were expecting a Messiah, a Son of David, who would restore the kingdom to its original glory.

No doubt that expectation was heightened when the Magi arrived in Jerusalem, saying they were searching for a newborn king of the Jews (Matt 2:2). King Herod the Great was disturbed that he might have a rival nearby, so he plotted to eliminate the perceived threat to his reign by asking the

Magi to report back to him when they located the infant king (Matt 2:8). Jewish scholars in Jerusalem told Herod the promised child would be born in Bethlehem according to prophecy, so when the Magi failed to report back, Herod simply slaughtered all baby boys under two years of age born in Bethlehem (Matt 2:16).

What we understand from these events is that the kingdom of God focuses on Jesus himself as king, and that his coming reign is seen as a threat by earthly rulers. Satan understood that Jesus' goal was nothing less than to become ruler of all kingdoms in the world, so he tempted Jesus, offering to give him those kingdoms if he would just bow down and worship him (Matt 4:8-9). Apparently Satan claimed that those kingdoms were his, and certainly Herod's conduct indicated that Satan was in charge in Palestine.

Jesus never intended to go into an alliance with Satan to achieve his goals; rather he would enter into a life and death struggle with Satan for dominance. Jesus never presented himself as an earthly king in his ministry, however, but more as a rabbi with a small band of disciples. In its early stage, at least, Jesus' kingdom was spiritual and was clearly not a direct threat to regular kingdoms, nor was it anything like them. This disappointed many would-be followers.

Jesus' message was just the same as John the Baptist's: "Repent, for the kingdom of heaven is near" (Matt 4:17). In the Sermon on the Mount, Jesus expanded on the spiritual nature of the kingdom, saying, "Unless your righteousness surpasses that of the Pharisees and the teachers of the law, you will certainly not enter the kingdom of heaven" (Matt 5:20). He defined the kingdom in what we know as the "Lord's prayer" in Matthew 6:10 when he taught his disciples to pray, "Your kingdom come, your will be done on earth, as it is in heaven." Using the parallelism of Hebrew poetry, where the second line often restates the first one in different words, the kingdom is simply where God's will is being done on earth as it is in heaven. That should include the church, but I was taught that we need no longer pray "Your kingdom come," because the church is now here. The real question is whether God's will is actually being done on earth. Certainly it is not being followed consistently, neither in Israel in Jesus' day nor in the church today.

Jesus continued in the Sermon on the Mount, "Not everyone who says to me, 'Lord, Lord,' will enter the kingdom of heaven, but only he who does the will of my Father who is in heaven" (Matt 7:21). Obedience to the king is clearly expected in God's kingdom. It is difficult for a committed individual to let God reign completely, much less an entire community. In an encounter with a Roman centurion in Matthew 8, Jesus praised the Gentile's faith in him as far outshining what he witnessed among his fellow Jews. He added, "Many will come from the east and the west, and will take their places at the feast with Abraham, Isaac and Jacob in the kingdom of heaven. But the subjects of the kingdom will be thrown outside, into the darkness, where there will be weeping and gnashing of teeth" (Matt 8:11-12). Predicting that outsiders to God's promises will flood into the kingdom, Jesus also prophesied that those who should be inside will end up losing their rightful places at the table with the Jewish patriarchs. It all centers on our reaction to Jesus and whether we are really his disciples. The Jewish community in general did not accept Jesus, but some individuals did.

Usually it is not so much a territory that is transformed by the gospel as it is hearts of believers. But it can happen, as I saw in Magobbo, that a whole community begins to be transformed by the simple preaching of and obedience to the gospel. In that case, even non-Christians feel the strong influence of the gospel and their community values start to change. Those who feel uncomfortable with the changes still go their own way, but they no longer represent the norm.

Those who reject the gospel may even do their best to undermine it. In places like Africa, they may well resort to witchcraft to curse evangelists like Isaac in their efforts to restore their original culture and beliefs to the neighborhood. Then the kingdom means a struggle for hearts and minds. In Jesus' ministry, the Pharisees and teachers of the law attacked his teaching and popularity by attributing his miracles to Satan (Matt 12:24). Jesus replied to this accusation with some important words: "If I drive out demons by the Spirit of God, then the kingdom of God has come upon you" (Matt 12:28). This is practically another definition of the kingdom—that the arrival of the kingdom of God results in the removal of demonic activity. It is in this sense that the concept of the kingdom has the most meaning for me in the context of mission work in Africa.

Spiritual warfare is the clash of two kingdoms: God's and Satan's. Even though it draws its imagery from military clashes, it should remain spiritual. For example, Paul says in 2 Corinthians 10:4, "The weapons we fight with are not the weapons of the world. On the contrary, they have divine power to demolish strongholds." The strongholds he is referring to were within the Corinthian church, as the context makes clear. Satan likes nothing better than to infiltrate the church and tie up its God-given agenda. Probably we can say that the church itself is the central battleground in spiritual warfare.

Who Needs a Missionary?

In Africa (and elsewhere), sometimes the spiritual battle can become physical. To cite two examples, I once witnessed a baptismal service where candidates were lined up on the shore of a river, while the baptizer, Tennyson Todd, called them one by one into the water. When Tennyson, a short wiry man, was about to baptize a younger and stronger man, the youth suddenly went berserk. He writhed in Tennyson's grip and attempted to drag him under the water. I was watching on the opposite bank and immediately thought the younger man was trying to drown Tennyson, so I started to run over to try to help Tennyson. Meanwhile, Tennyson was able to tear himself free from the other man's grasp. The youth then ran screaming to the shore and another youth who had also been waiting in line for baptism joined him in screaming loudly, while both took off into the forest. By this time everyone was so upset that there were no more baptisms done that day.

The other case involved two evangelists who were trying to exorcise a demon manifesting in a teenage girl. This happened during a church service in a hut where I was also present to witness the event. During the prayer time for those responding to the message, the girl fell down and rolled over and over toward the door. The two evangelists grabbed her and tried to restrain her so they could pray for her release from demonization. Yet she was strong enough to keep both men, as strong and powerful as they were, occupied for two straight hours, physically holding her to prevent her escape out the door. Throughout the time, she continued to roll on the floor, heading toward the door. Finally, when both men were literally soaked in sweat from their exertions, her demon-possession ended and she was able to bring objects she had been keeping that were dedicated to ancestral spirits. These were then burned publically to release their power over her.

In both cases, the real spiritual battle did not only reside in the individuals who had the strange behavior, but also in the churches where they were. I doubt if any physical force would have been necessary if the church people had been in line with God's will. In the first case, the young man who was in the water was not a true candidate for baptism, as he still followed ancestral spirits, but he had joined the line in order to keep his friend from being baptized, and it worked. If the local church leaders had simply prepared their candidates better for baptism and then allowed only those prepared to enter the water, the whole confusing situation could have been avoided.

In the second case, the men who were trying to exorcise the demon from the girl were probably not as prepared as Isaac usually was to face

Transforming the Community

demonic activity. Isaac always tried to avoid disturbances in church services. Certainly Jesus never had to wrestle with a demon-possessed person, as merely a word sufficed to expel the evil spirit. In this I also indict myself, as I had no better answer to this episode of demonization than to pray for the girl during her two-hour bout with the evangelists. What little I know about handling demonic activity, I learned from Africans, but I am a long way from handling demons with a simple word as Jesus did.

Jesus dealt with the mystery of the kingdom that he represented in a series of kingdom parables, such as those in Matthew 13. He seemed to be trying to show that the glorious kingdom people were expecting him to usher in would not be what they actually got. Rather it would be a subtle kingdom that defied the norm, so it had to be described in word pictures. The parables in Matthew 13 are mostly agricultural images. They speak of planting seeds in various soils that produce differing amounts of harvest, planting seeds that Satan infiltrates with weeds that look like good crops, or planting the tiniest of seeds that become large trees. The kingdom is also likened to a hidden treasure or a pearl of great value that a man happens to find, or to a fishing net that drags in all manner of fish, some good and some bad.

The kingdom parables emphasize the spiritual nature of the kingdom. It would be a ministry of seed-planting that ultimately results in a great harvest, but that would take time. Satan would try his best to disrupt the harvest by mixing in weeds with good crops, or bad fish in with the good. But God's kingdom would grow and dominate Satan's in the end. The parables are really about the abundant harvest to be reaped at the end of time, when God's kingdom will become all-consuming. It is ultimately a pearl of great price, but it always surprises us that it is so, because of its humble beginnings.

The parable that paints a picture of Isaac's ministry for me is Mark 4:26-29. Jesus says that the kingdom is like a farmer planting seed that grows night and day without the planter understanding why and how. "All by itself the soil produces grain—first the stalk, then the head, then the full kernel in the head" (Mark 4:28). I used the words "All by Itself" in the title of this book because it captures the power of the gospel to produce a lasting harvest on its own, without human ingenuity. The growth comes in stages, representing more and more visible fruitfulness, but starting small and insignificant. God has somehow decided to let it be this way.

Who Needs a Missionary?

Isaac shows part of his bountiful harvest.

Social Improvement

While I tend to think of the kingdom concept from the gospels as meaning spiritual warfare where God conquers Satan's domain, others have used "kingdom" to mean various other things. For example, Walter Rauschenbusch interpreted Jesus' use of "kingdom of God" in terms of what came to be known as the "Social Gospel." Early in the twentieth century, the meaning of the "kingdom of God" had taken several different directions. Rauschenbusch summarized, "To the ordinary reader of the Bible, 'inheriting the kingdom of God' simply means being saved and going to heaven."[1] Others viewed the kingdom as a future millennium, while still others equated it with the visible church.[2] All these interpretations, according to Rauschenbusch, had resulted from the gospel moving out of Palestine into the Greek world, where the term "kingdom" became spiritualized with no remaining reference to the nation of Israel.[3]

Rauschenbusch stressed that Jewish expectations of the kingdom in the time of Jesus "involved the restoration of Israel as a nation to outward independence, security, and power, such as it had under the Davidic

1. Rauschenbusch, *Christianity and the Social Crisis*, 54–55.
2. Ibid., 55.
3. Ibid.

Transforming the Community

kings."[4] That included "social justice, prosperity, and happiness" as well as national purity and holiness.[5] He maintained that Jesus must have used the term in the same way, saying, "If he did not mean by it [kingdom of God] the substance of what they meant by it, it was a mistake to use the term."[6] Rauschenbusch noted, however, "It is very possible that he [Jesus] seriously modified and corrected the popular conception."[7] For example, he was opposed to violence and bloodshed to accomplish his kingdom objectives.

For his part, Rauschenbusch interpreted the kingdom of God in social terms:

> The kingdom of God is still a collective conception, involving the whole social life of man. It is not a matter of saving human atoms, but of saving the social organism. It is not a matter of getting individuals to heaven, but of transforming life on earth into the harmony of heaven.[8]

Indeed, he maintained that "the essential purpose of Christianity was to transform human society into the kingdom of God by regenerating all human relationships and reconstituting them in accordance with the will of God."[9] This is the essence of what came to be known as the Social Gospel. The kingdom of God would be an ideal society on earth created by social improvement.

In writing of the transformation of the community around Magobbo, am I then referring to Isaac bringing in the kingdom of God in that area? Obviously not. For one thing, I don't think community transformation is his objective in the way that it was Rauschenbusch's; for another, I am under no illusions that Magobbo will remain a transformed community for the long term. There are still plenty of non-Christians and halfhearted Christians, not to mention the devil himself, that have other plans for the place. And even more importantly, the kingdom of God belongs to God and he brings it in his own time in his own way. In the book of Daniel, the picture of the kingdom is the "rock cut out of a mountain, but not by human hands" (Dan 2:45), which smashed earthly kingdoms to pieces. The real kingdom of God is not ushered in by human achievement.

4. Ibid., 56–57.
5. Ibid., 57.
6. Ibid.
7. Ibid.
8. Ibid., 65.
9. Ibid., xxiii.

Who Needs a Missionary?

In his discourse on the gospel of the kingdom, George Eldon Ladd stated, "Our responsibility is not to save the world. We are not required to transform This Age."[10] According to Matthew 24, "there will be wars and troubles, persecutions, and martyrdoms until the very end."[11] Yet we have the gospel of the kingdom to take to the world: "The forces of the Evil One are assaulting the people of God, but the gospel of the kingdom is assaulting the kingdom of Satan."[12] Ladd concluded, "Final victory will be achieved only by the return of Christ. There is no room for an unqualified optimism."[13] Isaac simply does battle with the forces of evil using the gospel without deliberately trying to transform society.

When we Western Christians think about socioeconomic improvement today, we tend to imagine how philanthropists, the United Nations' Millennial Goals, or the forces of globalization are making life better for the world's poor. But those secular forces are not always benign or neutral. For example, one initiative I mentioned in Chapter 4 that came from us missionaries to help Isaac economically was to assist him to grow cotton. At the time, Zimbabwe was encouraging and helping small-scale farmers to join in the international cotton markets. All it took to get started was fertilizer, seeds, and pesticides, as most farmers already had plows and other basic farming tools.

Until globalization made inroads into the Zambezi Valley, Tonga people had little need for cash, as they grew only what they consumed. With globalization, they began to need money for such things as sugar, tea, bread, cooking oil, matches, and school fees. Cotton was a promising way to get one paycheck a year to cover not only those kinds of costs, but also to build more permanent houses and to buy durable animal-drawn carts. For a number of years, cotton became Isaac's main source of income. It enabled him to build a better home for his family, pay school fees for all his children, and improve his farming methods. It appeared to be the right crop for that part of the country and the answer for job creation and income.

So I was surprised when Isaac told me he had quit cotton farming temporarily. He gave two main reasons: first was the deteriorating economic situation in Zimbabwe that made it more and more difficult to transport cotton to gins, and to be treated fairly once the cotton was delivered.

10. Ladd, "Gospel of the Kingdom," 75.
11. Ibid.
12. Ibid., 76.
13. Ibid.

Transforming the Community

Zimbabwe's gin towns had become home to lots of gangsters and swindlers. But second was an unexpected byproduct of globalization itself: American government subsidies of its own cotton farmers kept the world price of cotton artificially low, putting millions of African small-scale farmers out of work. World markets, it turns out, are not a level playing field.

But world markets did not concern Isaac; his real concern was spreading the gospel. He would continue his work regardless of the drawbacks from globalization. If it could supply jobs, good and well, but if not, the Tonga people could always fall back on subsistence farming, which kept them alive for millennia before the advent of globalization. Isaac, like many Tongas, started to grow smaller quantities of cotton just to pay the main bills, rather than rely on it for livelihood.

Western Christians also imagine that wealthy Christians should bail out poorer ones in the developing world so they can enjoy a better life. That is the main premise of John Rowell's book, *To Give or Not To Give?*, that proposes a new Christian "Marshall Plan"[14] to pour Western funds into poorer places to improve standards of living. While it is true that Western Christians need to be more generous, there are also major flaws in Rowell's approach that are addressed in Steve Corbett and Brian Fikkert's book, *When Helping Hurts*.

Corbett and Fikkert emphasize how rich and poor both have marred relationships with God, self, others, and creation.[15] Despite the poverty of such broken relationships, the wealthy tend to assume god-complexes toward the materially poor. On the other hand, the poor tend to have inferiority complexes that are reinforced by the kind of condescending poverty-alleviation programs designed for them.[16] Thus the attempt by wealthy outsiders to uplift the poor often tends to do more harm than good. The result is that "when North American Christians do attempt to alleviate poverty, the methods used often do considerable harm to both the materially poor and the materially non-poor."[17]

Corbett and Fikkert say that "the first step in overcoming our god-complexes is to repent of the health and wealth gospel."[18] By that, they mean we need to reject the automatic assumption that God rewards faithfulness

14. Rowell, *To Give or Not To Give?*, 141–45.
15. Corbett and Fikkert, *When Helping Hurts*, 61.
16. Ibid., 65.
17. Ibid., 28.
18. Ibid., 69.

with material prosperity. And likewise, we cannot assume that poverty is always the result of unfaithfulness. Such assumptions tend to increase the harm caused by the interaction of god-complexes and inferiority complexes. Those who assume they are the saviors of the poor act as though their ideas for social improvement are God-ordained, while the recipients of the generosity tend to seethe with resentment even while being handed things for free. Both indicate by these attitudes how broken and poor are their relationships with God and others.

If wealthy believers could be the source of all blessings for the poor, then God would certainly have used this method in Bible days. However, the message of Scripture is that God prefers to use unlikely sources of blessing so that his name will be glorified instead of human achievement. Paul made this clear when he wrote, "God chose the lowly things of the world and the despised things—and things that are not—to nullify things that are, so that no one may boast before him" (1 Cor 1:28–29). This helps explain why Isaac was able to effect transformation with so few resources, because God was behind it. This is not to discard the generosity of those who have many possessions, since some of them were used to boost Isaac a little, but the key was that those resources could not explain the outcome that God finally brought.

Summary

How did a first-grade dropout like Isaac manage to transform his community in so many different ways? His case is unusual among our church members, but it deserves to be more the norm. So we must ask: How did this happen? I see three abiding principles:

1. A thorough conversion to Christ. When Isaac became a Christian, his thought processes and actions no longer resembled those of a spiritualist who lives in fear of evil spirits and seeks to manipulate the spirit world for personal advantage. His entire worldview changed deep down toward an active trust in God to protect and guide his family. Now he was no longer in bondage to forces that crippled his people's initiative. He was no longer afraid of what sorcerers and witches could do to him, so he could preach the gospel with assurance and boldness. He became a thorough Christian, not a half-hearted one who dabbled in both faiths.

Transforming the Community

2. A burning desire to share the new faith with his own people. Isaac left a job, where he was being promoted by his bosses for his dependability, in order to share his faith with his Tonga people in an area with no job security. His motive was simply that his own people were still in bondage as he had been, and he knew what freedom in Christ felt like. He entered into years of active spiritual warfare as he faced spiritualists who tried to shut down his work of spreading the gospel. But he did so willingly, for the sake of his people. No matter the personal cost, which was great, he was dedicated to his people.

3. Distance from outside resources. Local initiative is often swallowed up by well-meaning outsiders with great resources. In Isaac's case, he had chosen to serve God in such a remote and sometimes inaccessible region that outside help was simply not available most of the year. Other promising church leaders like Isaac did not produce such strong local initiative because they lived in closer proximity to missionaries like us. Isaac, on the other hand, had to develop all his talents by relying solely on God to provide necessities. He had to weather adversities by faith and in the process trained disciples who also showed great local initiative.

Isaac and Margaret with three sons and a daughter-in-law.

Who Needs a Missionary?

Scripture says, "The last shall be first" (Mark 10:31), and Isaac certainly illustrates how God often surprises us with the fruit coming from someone who seems insignificant. Given the chance, true transformation of spirit and community can come from local initiative that is dedicated to Christ.

8

Rebuilding the Walls

I have an indelible memory of a leaders' meeting held in Patse, near the border with Botswana, where various church leaders were given chapters of the book of Nehemiah to speak on. We wanted to hold this type of meeting outside Bulawayo, so rural folks could take advantage of strong Bible teaching without having to travel to the city. It was May 1990, and we borrowed a truck from a businessman friend who owned Willsgrove Farm near Esigodini and loaded it with both food and leaders for the two-hundred kilometer drive to Patse. Along the way, in the more remote places, we stopped and picked up firewood from the roadside to have plenty of fuel for cooking and evening warmth. It was the cold season, and temperatures could easily drop below freezing in that district at night.

It did indeed turn cold, but we still held the meetings outdoors to take advantage of the sun's warmth even in winter, basking like lizards while hearing God's word expounded. This turned out to be the most memorable of all these regular leaders' meetings, mainly because of a connection between Isaac and Nehemiah, which none of us knew about. Ironically, we had not even chosen Isaac to speak, not realizing he was deeply interested in Nehemiah, but had rather chosen nine other speakers, mostly from the educated urban church membership. Isaac stole the show, however, when he was asked to do a short meditation. He opened by saying, "I see myself as Nehemiah, trying to rebuild the broken walls at my home." He related how God had made Nehemiah central in his thinking, and he proceeded to unlock the thought of Nehemiah as if he himself were a character in God's ancient drama. It was electrifying.

Who Needs a Missionary?

At a Bulawayo leaders' meeting in July 2013. Isaac is in the front row on the left.

Prior to this meeting, I had been using Alan Redpath's book *Victorious Christian Service* about Nehemiah to teach some city leaders about Christian leadership, and it is this book that provides an outline for principles I will mention in this chapter, since they are the same ones that we used in Patse to divide up the topics among the leaders. For the first time, we were allowing rural Africans to give us the meat of God's word from their own unique perspective. As they tend to do, Africans interpret by placing themselves in the Bible story, and that is what makes it riveting.

Chapter 1 of Nehemiah opens with a report coming from Jerusalem to Nehemiah, who is in exile in Persia, about the disgrace of his home town: "The wall of Jerusalem is broken down, and its gates have been burned with fire" (Neh 1:3). Isaac said he had learned about the "broken walls" of his home of Magobbo, and this distressed him just as it distressed Nehemiah. His response was the same: "When I heard these things, I sat down and wept. For some days I mourned and fasted and prayed before the God of heaven" (Neh 1:4). Redpath says, "Before you begin any service for the Master, I urge you first of all to survey the ruins around you."[1]

That is how Isaac's burden began. Such a deep burden is essential for someone to carry in order to serve fervently in God's cause. Isaac was

1. Redpath, *Victorious Christian Service*, 20.

Rebuilding the Walls

appalled at the condition of his people after his own eyes had been opened by the gospel. In their case, the broken walls meant that Satan could come and go as he pleased, since he ruled the place. There was no protection against humanity's greatest enemy. Redpath says that the needs of a lost world must become "a specific burden in my soul for one particular piece of work which God would have me do."[2] Prayer and fasting put the potential leaders in a position of recognizing how dependent they are on God before God can use them to full potential in a specific cause.

After prayer, Nehemiah determined to ask the king of Persia for leave to go rebuild the walls of Jerusalem. He had a job of considerable prestige and trust, being cupbearer to King Artaxerxes (Neh 2:1). This meant he was allowed to hand the most powerful ruler on earth his cup of wine, and the king knew it was safe to drink. He could not have considered asking such a favor of this king without establishing a good reputation with him first. Similarly, Isaac had built a strong reputation for honesty and hard work, being elevated to foreman of all the Wolhuters' workers on the chicken farm. He too decided to ask for leave to go preach the gospel in Magobbo, only in his case it would be a permanent relocation. It was not a request that any employer would normally like to grant, because it meant losing a trusted man who would be hard to replace.

Artaxerxes granted not only the leave that Nehemiah requested, but also helped cover the expenses of rebuilding the walls and provided him a military escort to Jerusalem. Likewise the Wolhuters actively supported Isaac's venture of faith, knowing he was called by God for this new phase of life. They visited Isaac in Magobbo shortly after he settled there and continued to encourage him and pray for his work. Up to now, Isaac always asks me how the Wolhuters are doing; the bond they had long ago still holds.

But upon arrival in Jerusalem, Nehemiah found that enemies of his work "were very much disturbed that someone had come to promote the welfare of the Israelites" (Neh 2:10). He would face continuous opposition from foes like Sanballat, Tobiah, and Geshem, who tried every trick they could think of to slow down or stop progress on the rebuilding of the walls. These antagonists were half-Jews or non-Jews and desperately wanted the Jews to remain powerless and defenseless. Isaac also faced immediate opposition, even from his own family, since the uncle in whose village he was living was in *inyanga*. Numerous others also opposed Isaac's work for various reasons and tried to bewitch him to make him change his emphasis

2. Ibid., 31.

on the gospel or stop preaching altogether. The entrenched powers in Magobbo had no interest in the gospel spreading, but rather fervently wanted ancient Tonga culture, based on the fear of evil spirits and reverence for spirit practitioners, to continue unchallenged as it had for centuries.

The first thing that Nehemiah did when he arrived in Jerusalem was to carry out a night inspection of the true condition of the broken walls (Neh 2:12–16). He needed to see the situation for himself, without relying on others' reports alone. He needed to "count the cost" (Luke 14:28–9) before launching into action. Only then did he seek to mobilize the citizens of Jerusalem behind his efforts to rebuild. Isaac did not have any other Christians to mobilize, since he was starting from scratch. Nevertheless, he needed to see the facts of the situation for himself and he did this by meeting with those interested in the gospel during his leave days as he was phasing out of his job with the Wolhuters. In this way, he gained a clear picture of what he would be facing before he actually moved to Magobbo. He had already seen the demonic activity he would need to combat in order to make any progress. It would be so challenging that he would need to rely totally on God through prayer and fasting on a regular basis.

Once Nehemiah had mobilized the Jews living in Jerusalem to take part in reconstruction of the various sections of the wall, his enemies responded by asking, "What is this you are doing? . . . Are you rebelling against the king?" (Neh 2:19). Here is their first attempt at intimidation, a practice that is also widely used in Africa to prevent any change in the status quo. While Nehemiah had the full confidence of the king, his enemies insinuated that the rebuilding of the walls was treasonous. He replied, "The God of heaven will give us success. We his servants will start rebuilding, but as for you, you have no share in Jerusalem or any claim or historic right to it" (Neh 2:20). The answer seems harsh, even callous, but Nehemiah had already sized up his enemies' motivation. They were going to oppose him out of envy no matter what happened.

Isaac had to be as determined as Nehemiah in the face of opposition. Having grown up in the Tonga culture, he knew intimately what drove people to do what they did. Now he had found a better way than what he grew up with. He had to tell them the hard truth that the way of Christ is so far superior to traditional African religion that he could never water it down to suit them. The fact is that walking with Jesus is better than any other way of life and we need to tell people so, even if it seems harsh to them. Both Nehemiah and Isaac were uncompromising about their faith and their calling and didn't mind telling people so. However, the gospel promise is available even to the most diehard spiritualist or secularist who decides to repent, whereas the Jewish covenant was not as open to non-Jews. While telling people hard truths they may not want to hear, we need not alienate them, but rather invite them in to meet Christ. The important thing is that they should see a clear difference between their old beliefs and following Christ.

In Nehemiah's case, the harsh tone only increased the hostility and deception coming from his opponents. Sanballat began with ridicule: "What are those feeble Jews doing? Will they restore their wall? . . . Can they bring those stones back to life from those heaps of rubble—burned as they are?" (Neh 4:2). Tobiah added, "What they are building—if even a fox climbed up on it, he would break down their wall of stones!" (Neh 4:3). As Redpath noted, the world tends to pay attention to headlines and big projects, but pours scorn on what appears insignificant: "Even Christian people seem to believe that to accomplish anything for God you must prove to the world that you can put on something big."[3] We are enamored with celebrities to the extent that even Christian gatherings are considered incomplete without them.

Isaac, on the other hand, is a first-grade dropout who was beginning from scratch to plant a church in his home where there had never been one before. He had no financial backing or big names to bring with him. He must have seemed less than significant when he arrived with his small family—just a local boy returning home, which usually meant he had failed to make it big elsewhere. In Africa, however, the presence of white people accompanying an African often seems like a statement of exceptional backing. White people are regarded as powerful and wealthy; they can either be seen as game-changers or as threats. In Isaac's case, the presence of white people like the Wolhuters and us missionaries did not happen often enough to make much of a statement, any more than Nehemiah's backing by the distant King Artaxerxes seemed to have helped him avoid opposition in Jerusalem. Sanballat had already threatened to report Nehemiah as a rebel to the king and he would threaten this again.

So what was Nehemiah's reaction to this taunting scorn? After his customary prayer, telling God that "we are despised" (Neh 4:4), Nehemiah just kept on building till the wall was half completed. Redpath notes how, under Nehemiah's leadership, the citizens of Jerusalem "simply concentrated on

---

3. Ibid., 72.

doing the thing that God had called them to do."[4] Isaac likewise ignored opposition in his determination to complete the mission God gave him. Distraction is a frequent and often effective tactic of the devil to get God's people off track, but neither Nehemiah nor Isaac allowed that to happen. Single-mindedness was definitely required!

Once Nehemiah and his people had reached the halfway stage it might have seemed that it would be smooth sailing the rest of the way, but that was not the case. Redpath calls halfway "the hardest place of all."[5] That is because after coming a long way, when strength and determination are depleted, the realization sets in that there is just as much left to finish. The initial spurt of enthusiasm has long since evaporated, but the remaining task is still massive. Just as strength ebbs, the enemies decide to attack. Sanballat, Tobiah, and Geshem became so alarmed and angry that the walls of Jerusalem were going up quickly that "they all plotted together to come and fight against Jerusalem" (Neh 4:8).

In Isaac's case, I am not sure what represents the arrival at the halfway stage, since he is still engaged in "rebuilding the walls." Nonetheless, there must have been many times when, despite accomplishing a lot, doubt set in about the possibility of finishing all that God gave him to do. The deaths of his oldest daughter and of Francis Mudimba, his right-hand man, must have been such times. His own serious illnesses must have made him wonder if his time was up before he had finished God's work. Certainly the frontal attack made by his opponents when they accused him of making a girl pregnant may have come when he was vulnerable to doubts about his mission. The very family from which the girl came, the extended family of those he had taken in when they became Christians and lost their income as rainmakers, turned against him, saying he had taken advantage of a teenager sheltering in his own home. But there is no indication that Isaac ever thought of throwing in the towel, even when his own integrity was under such intense scrutiny by people both inside and outside the church.

How did Nehemiah respond to threats of active violence? "We prayed to our God and posted a guard day and night to meet this threat" (Neh 4:9). He took the threats seriously but still did not stop the work. His workers, however, were discouraged: "The strength of the laborers is giving out, and there is so much rubble that we cannot rebuild the wall" (Neh 4:10). Some of the Jews themselves predicted a bad outcome, saying, "Wherever

4. Ibid., 75.
5. Ibid., 95.

Rebuilding the Walls

you turn, they will attack us" (Neh 4:12). Sensing that despair was creeping into the ranks of his followers, Nehemiah had to strengthen defenses and encourage the workers, saying, "Remember the Lord, who is great and awesome, and fight for your brothers, your sons and your daughters, your wives and your homes" (Neh 4:14).

Redpath noted, "Everything was at stake in the battle; everything that was dear to them depended upon the outcome."[6] So it was with Isaac; the battle he had joined was a conflict between two opposite worldviews. If traditional religion was right, Isaac would have to back down or leave; if Christ was true and real, then spiritualism would have to allow a new and potentially stronger worldview into its domain. Redpath asked, "Should sheer satanic pressure bring fear into the church? Never!"[7] That is how Isaac felt, but others were not so sure, and these were the ones who allowed fear to enter the Christian ranks. Just as Nehemiah was faced with pessimists among his followers, so was Isaac; even his first convert, his cousin Mpendulo, gave up and reverted to spiritualism. The battle proved costly and demanded strong leadership.

In Nehemiah's case, half his people continued to build the walls, while the other half kept watch (Neh 4:16). Even the builders had weapons close at hand. And Nehemiah was the rallying point, as "the man who sounded the trumpet stayed with me" (Neh 4:18). Round the clock vigilance was required at this delicate stage; those who worked on the wall in the daylight also acted as guards at night (Neh 4:22). Nehemiah didn't even take time to change clothes at night (Neh 4:23). This kind of determined leadership kept the workers going when fatigue and despair could have crept into their ranks. Isaac was careful to keep Jesus as the rallying point in all that he did. He knew that while he might fail, Jesus never would if only people could come to know and trust him.

While most of the initial opposition against Nehemiah came from the traditional enemies of the Jews, the Samaritans, opposition also began to arise from within the ranks of the Jews themselves. Quarrels broke out over treatment of the poor among them. Those Jews hit hardest by famine ended up selling their sons and daughters into slavery to fellow Jews (Neh 5:5). As Redpath noted, "There were people who were prepared to take advantage of the situation"[8] regarding the food shortage. They were ready to profit

---

6. Ibid., 104.
7. Ibid., 99.
8. Ibid., 110.

from other people's misfortune by granting high-interest loans with the expectation that the borrowers would default and have to sell their children into slavery.

Nehemiah handled the situation by pinpointing the problem: "You are exacting usury from your own countrymen!" (Neh 5:7). This practice was expressly forbidden in the Law of Moses. In Leviticus 25:35–46, Moses stated that fellow Jews were not to be charged interest on loans, nor to be sold into slavery. The reason: "Because the Israelites are my servants, whom I brought out of Egypt, they must not be sold as slaves" (Lev 25:42). God had gone to great lengths to redeem his people from Egyptian slavery, so he had no intention of allowing the perpetuation of their slavery just because times were hard. Nehemiah rightly called a general meeting of all concerned, because the issue amounted to a breach of the covenant with God!

Although Isaac did not deal with a problem of equal magnitude, he did run into problems related to benevolence. The Wolhuters brought a load of used clothing to distribute to Christians on one of their visits to Isaac's home. As mentioned earlier, this caused Isaac some headaches because of accusations of favoritism if one person received articles of clothing better than someone else. In particular, since Isaac ministered mostly to women at first, it appeared to their husbands that Isaac was trying to seduce them with gifts of clothing! To avert this kind of accusation, Isaac simply hung the clothing up and let church members take one item of their own choosing, eliminating favoritism as much as possible.

Issues of poverty among Christians even hit the early church in Acts 6:1. The apostles had to use all their wisdom to avert a crisis in the church over racial prejudice, since the poorer people were all Greek-speaking foreigners. In Nehemiah's case, he forced the wealthier Jews to promise to stop charging interest on loans and to return any property they had already confiscated from poorer Jews (Neh 5:11). Beyond compulsion, Nehemiah also had to live the way he wanted other wealthy Jews to live, without the usual perks that governors had come to expect. Whereas previous governors had taxed people heavily to support their privileged lifestyles, Nehemiah said, "But out of reverence for God I did not act like that" (Neh 6:15). He worked single-mindedly on the wall and did not use his position as governor to enrich himself or his men (Neh 6:16).

Getting money for ministry, while permissible, is a potential trap; Isaac avoided this pitfall by supporting himself throughout. Redpath noted that God's work "is going to be attacked far more by internal dissension than by outward opposition, and the basis of trouble is usually a general acceptance of a wrong standard of life."[9] The temptation to seek wealthy benefactors for ministry can quickly lead to corruption and can pervert the gospel itself. Poor Christians, who are the vast majority of the world's Christians, are particularly susceptible to this temptation. The apostle Paul recognized the dangers of preaching for a salary: "What then is my reward? Just this: that in preaching the gospel I may offer it free of charge, and so not make use of my rights in preaching it" (1 Cor 9:18). Isaac followed the same practice.

No sooner had Nehemiah reined in the greed of wealthy Jews than he faced renewed opposition from the Samaritans. This time they tried a new tactic: they pretended to be concerned for Nehemiah and offered friendly talks to sort out differences (Neh 6:2). Gone were the threats and ridicule; now they offered friendship. All the while, they really only intended to slow down his progress toward rebuilding the walls of Jerusalem. Nehemiah saw through their ruse and sent a terse message to Sanballat and Tobiah: "I am carrying on a great project and cannot go down. Why should the work stop while I leave it and go down to you?" (Neh 6:3). His wily opponents then tried another tactic: they pretended to be alarmed by gossip about Nehemiah's intentions. They claimed that reports were heading to King Artaxerxes that Nehemiah was planning to make himself king of Judah! Yet they said their own intentions were to spare Nehemiah embarrassment or worse (Neh 6:6–7). Again Nehemiah sent a brief message: "Nothing like what you are saying is happening: you are just making it up out of your head" (Neh 6:8).

Redpath says, "If the world cannot persuade the Christian to compromise, it will begin to spread rumors about him and misrepresent his motives."[10] This happened many times to Isaac as detailed earlier. Compromise often seems the easiest course to take as continuous opposition takes a toll. Even Nehemiah had to pray: "Now strengthen my hands" (Neh 6:9). Shortly after that prayer, Nehemiah faced a new and dangerous situation that could easily have blindsided him. A person he thought he could trust urged him to shut himself inside the temple to escape an assassination plot (Neh 6:10). Nehemiah realized that the man had only been hired by Sanballat and Tobiah to make him seem like a coward to his own followers; he replied, "Should a man like me run away? Or should one like me go into the temple to save his life? I will not go!" (Neh 6:11).

9. Ibid., 112.
10. Ibid., 129.

Who Needs a Missionary?

All these were various forms of distraction that Nehemiah's enemies planned in order to stop the rebuilding of the walls. Redpath says, "No man can lead a work of God if he allows himself to be governed by what other people think."[11] On occasion I have heard Isaac say, "I don't trust anyone." That statement has troubled me because it seems that trusting others is essential for their growth and fellowship, but in the context of continuous opposition from without and within, I can at least understand that Isaac trusted God's call on his life more than any advice or plans he got from others, including missionaries. I believe that Isaac represented in some ways as key a leader as Nehemiah who entered the crucible for God. If he could have been made to stumble by any means, then God's work might have suffered or died, simply because there were so few other high quality leaders at the time.

The result of Nehemiah's steadfast determination to keep on building despite all the scorn, threats, and intrigue of the Samaritans, as well as all the temptations from insiders, was that the walls of Jerusalem were completed in a mere fifty-two days (Neh 6:15). Beyond that, "all our enemies lost their self-confidence, because they realized that this work had been done with the help of our God" (Neh 6:16). One might have thought that Nehemiah could settle into a routine career as governor, later retiring in a blaze of glory for his achievements, or perhaps he might feel free to return to his life as the king's cupbearer. But he knew the main work was still to come. Building with bricks is much easier than building a people who know and trust God.

Similarly, Isaac knew he had a long way to go even after building a church building and starting some other branch churches. Even after he had baptized dozens of followers of Christ, the main work still lay ahead. Converts have to be turned into disciples, a crucial step that is often forgotten or neglected. Redpath notes, "The great moment of achievement or success in Christian work is perhaps one of the most dangerous moments in a man's life."[12] He adds, "There is no experience in our Christian life, no matter how exhilarating or triumphant, which imparts to us strength for the future."[13] In other words, there is never a good reason to let our guard down as if we have arrived. As long as we are on earth, we remain in need of God's grace. We constantly need to be exposed to God's word. So Nehemiah

11. Ibid., 130.
12. Ibid., 137.
13. Ibid., 138.

Rebuilding the Walls

held an outdoor Scripture lesson for all inhabitants of Jerusalem and the surrounding area.

Nehemiah brought in another outstanding leader, Ezra the scribe, to lead the assembled Jews in reading and expounding the basis of their faith in the Torah (Neh 8:2–3). The immediate result of this unusual day was deep conviction of sin. People began weeping as they heard the Scripture (Neh 8:9). Redpath commented, "This day of great victory was also a day of deep conviction resulting in sadness of heart as they discovered how serious had been their failure in the light of God's word."[14] It is quite amazing that Nehemiah so soon took the people from the glory of completing the wall to despair over their sinfulness before God. But this was necessary soul therapy.

Isaac always welcomed chances for his people to get special Bible teaching. By the same token, he was unusual in that he also wanted his people to participate in the teaching and not just be recipients. While most Africans were very compliant with foreign visitors' wishes, Isaac could also make some pointed requests. For example, when I brought a group of Americans on a visit and we asked to teach and preach, he willingly accepted, but he insisted that his own trainees should also have a chance to join in. As it turned out, the teaching and preaching from the Tongas was inspirational to us visitors. And Isaac made sure that his disciples got more chances to lead than the visitors! He remained fixed on building not only buildings but also young leaders for the future.

When Nehemiah saw the effect of the Scripture on the hearers, he consoled them, saying, "Go and enjoy choice food and sweet drinks, and send some to those who have nothing prepared. This day is sacred to the Lord. Do not grieve, for the joy of the Lord is your strength" (Neh 8:10). From there the people began to celebrate the upcoming Feast of Tabernacles by building booths (Neh 8:16–17). The revelation of Scripture had put them back in the picture of where they came from and whose they were, so there was need to celebrate with the rituals that commemorated the wilderness wanderings. And each day of the feast there was more Scripture reading by Ezra (Neh 8:18) to reinforce understanding and purpose in the people.

The leaders' meeting at Patse was something like the Bible readings that Ezra did in Jerusalem, although not nearly as long. Each selected leader was able to take a portion of Nehemiah such as those we have just discussed and expound it to the assembled Christians over a period of a few days. By

14. Ibid., 139.

relating Zimbabwean life to that of ancient Israel, local Christians could put themselves deeply into the narrative in ways unachievable otherwise. We are just as much God's chosen people through Jesus Christ as Israel! At Patse this led to something like a revival because the word of God showed ordinary Zimbabweans how important they are as God's children as well as the need to persevere through many trials. Isaac's presentation in particular showed just how parallel his life had been to Nehemiah's and how God used both men for his glory, but it was not nearly over yet for Isaac.

Neither was the revival over for Nehemiah after the days of Bible reading during the Feast of Tabernacles. In fact, according to Redpath, it was just beginning, because now the Jews began to get serious with God about confessing their sins. Redpath notes that Chapter 9 of Nehemiah is full of "the great principles of revival."[15] The first is "brokenheartedness,"[16] where the feasting gave way to fasting. Redpath noted, "Days of great joy in the Lord are always accompanied by days of great humiliation in ourselves."[17] In Zimbabwe, I have seen this principle in the practice of beginning the new year with ten days of fasting, right after all the celebrations of Christmas. While we celebrate the birth of our Savior with big meals and lots of fellowship, we begin each new year with sober reflection about our need for God. Although Isaac could enjoy a festive occasion as much as anyone, he also made fasting a regular part of his life to gain God's strength for ministry.

Redpath notes that the second principle of revival found in Nehemiah Chapter 9 is to reflect on God's goodness.[18] He has always been faithful although we are sinful, which is the third principle.[19] Hence the need for regular confession and renewal of our commitment to God, which is the fourth and final principle.[20] Redpath notes, "Revival is not simply an emotional upheaval—it leads to action."[21] In Nehemiah's case, those Jews who had settled in or around Jerusalem after the exile made a binding agreement to obey the laws of Moses. In particular, they publically promised to cease marrying foreigners who did not belong to God's people, to cease trading

---

15. Ibid., 153.
16. Ibid., 155.
17. Ibid., 156.
18. Ibid.
19. Ibid., 159.
20. Ibid., 162.
21. Ibid.

goods on the Sabbath Day, and to support the work of the priesthood and the temple financially (Neh 10:30–32).

The necessity for such dramatic times of confession and renewal is evident from the fact that the people's commitment to these vows waned after some time, especially during Nehemiah's absence when he left to report back to King Artaxerxes. Upon his return, Nehemiah had to enact more reforms to uphold the promises already made by the Jews! Isaac too knows that growth in God's work can never be taken for granted. It calls for regular repentance and reaffirmation of covenant promises. It calls for special times of dedication such as choirs marching around Jerusalem on top of the newly constructed walls (Neh 12:31). But above all it calls for dedicated leadership of people like Nehemiah. Isaac could have done no better than to model his life after such a determined and faithful leader.

Both Nehemiah and Isaac worked tirelessly to build not so much walls or buildings as people. When Isaac surveyed the ruins of his people's lives it had little to do with their mud huts or ways of farming; he was most concerned about their lives, attitudes, and future. They were living without God and had no real hope for the future, hence no real purpose for living other than to maintain centuries-old traditions. They could not see beyond the narrow confines of Tonga identity, living in the shadow of their ancestral spirits, and they had no global understanding of their role on planet earth. Worse yet, they were enslaved to fear of evil spirits and at the mercy of spirit practitioners who could manipulate them at will. They were just as much in bondage as any African slaves captured for sale to the Americas or to the Middle East.

Summary

While Isaac is now an old man by African standards, he is still devoted to producing strong disciples who will continue the work he started at Magobbo and beyond. "Rebuilding the walls" of Tonga life will remain his goal, but hopefully not his alone, as he passes the torch of leadership to a new generation. Just like Nehemiah, his "mentor," Isaac's life will be but a vapor, perhaps soon forgotten by most people, and it soon may even be hard to say that he had a permanent impact on Tonga life. But all he can do is live faithfully for God and train as many disciples as possible in this life. And that is the main work God gives to all of us.

Who Needs a Missionary?

One of my missions professors used to talk about the stages that God's leaders go through in life. The final stage he called "afterglow," a period when one becomes something like an elder statesman with a proven reputation. He always added, however, that many never reach that stage because of some failure or circumstance. Even in the Bible, few leaders attained such a satisfying state in this life. For most, afterglow is reserved for heaven, and it is doubtful if Isaac will experience it on earth. There is too much left to be done and too many forces arrayed against him, but I pray that he will persevere with the task God gave him until the end, and I expect that he will do just that.

Epilogue

When I tell people Isaac's story, they have several reactions. A common one for Americans is to offer to support him financially. That is not really what he desires or asks for. Some would like to meet him and some are simply amazed. When I wrote about him in an article for a mission magazine, the editors wanted to know how to duplicate what he has done. That question stumped me because it is not easy to copy what happened to Isaac. Among the Christian Zimbabweans we worked with over a period of two decades, there are many church leaders just as zealous as Isaac, many dedicated to working for God in adverse circumstances, and many who continue to be faithful up to the present. But the details of Isaac's life are in a league of their own, and worthy of telling. I chose to write about him because his story is unique. But the editors of the mission magazine wanted to know if there are reproducible principles readers can gain from his inspiring story. Frankly, I struggled to find those principles and the editors rejected the publication of the article.

Now I may have discovered the answer. In reading Timothy Tennent's excellent book, *Invitation to World Missions*, I found that he built on the work of Lamin Sanneh and Kwame Bediako (both African missiologists and theologians) to show a three-point progression of how God works in mission. In what Tennent calls the stage of *preparatio evangelica*, "God prepares people to receive the gospel before any missionary arrives."[1] Certainly that was the case with Isaac, since he had already begun to follow Christ as far as he knew how, before any missionary met him. And he was unusually open to the material in the Voice of Prophecy tract written in a language that he did not understand; yet he took it as the voice of God directed to him personally! How that can be duplicated I do not know, but it shows the power of God in preparing hearts.

---

1. Tennent, *Invitation to World Missions*, 71.

Who Needs a Missionary?

Isaac and I in 2013.

Tennent's second stage is the historic transmission of the gospel, especially content about the Savior, Jesus.[2] Here Tennent brings in the work of the existing church or mission to teach and disciple new converts. In this phase, the church is simply being the body of Christ, especially his mouthpiece, in explaining the way of salvation through Christ. And this body needs to be local, so that it speaks to the context of the outsider. In Isaac's case, you may recall that he rushed to buy his first Tonga Bible in order to learn about his new Savior; the Bible was only available because the body of Christ had translated and marketed it locally. Then Sandy Wolhuter played her part, even though she was only a new convert herself, introducing Isaac to the local body of Christ so that he could get the fellowship, teaching, baptism, and discipleship that he needed to be fruitful. The point of this stage is to begin a deepening relationship between the convert (Isaac) and the Savior.

Tennent's third stage is indigenous assimilation of the gospel, as the Holy Spirit imprints the gospel on people's hearts so they can use it in their own ministry in their own way.[3] All that Isaac was taught or saw in the lives of fellow Christians, he had to digest and use for himself. The point

2. Ibid., 72.
3. Ibid., 73.

Epilogue

of this stage is that the Holy Spirit has to help the convert to become a disciple. Or in the frame of reference of the parable of the soils, the Holy Spirit has to prepare the soil, removing rocks and weeds so that the seed of the gospel can sprout, bloom, and produce multiple new seeds. Surely it is in the hearts of men and women that we see a major difference in types of soils and hence a major difference in fruitfulness. Those more open to the leading of the Spirit will produce more fruit.

We often want to approach real life stories from the point of view of how to duplicate an exemplary life, when what is really needed is to learn how to open ourselves up to God's work. In Isaac's story, I ultimately see the power of God to work with seemingly insignificant clay to produce something fine and beautiful. So I think the story is more about God than it is about Isaac. Some things are impossible to engineer without God!

Every story about the spread of the gospel has a human and a divine side. From the human side comes a note in passing: in 2013, as I was finishing the manuscript for this work, I met Isaac in Zimbabwe. In his usual unassuming way he explained that the church in Kalonga that I wrote about in Chapter 7 had broken away from direct fellowship with the rest of the churches he had started. He could not explain all the reasons; it was painful for both of us, because we had long known the leaders and were surprised by their action. As I said in that chapter, one can never predict how things will go on earth, for better or worse. It is certainly not all pure progress in one direction.

Now Isaac has another challenge to deal with, and that is how spiritual warfare goes on earth. Nevertheless, what keeps Isaac going is the knowledge that God is in charge of the overall process, that Jesus is still with him, and that the Holy Spirit is still at work. As uneven as is our progress here, God will see it through in his way and in his time. Isaac's story is really about God's promises and faithfulness. It is about the work of the whole Trinity in mission to accomplish God's purposes. It is about "the foolishness of God" being "wiser than man's wisdom" (1 Cor 1:25). Isaac's story confirms the verses: "God chose the lowly things of this world and the despised things—and the things that are not—to nullify the things that are, so that no one may boast before him" (1 Cor 1:28–29).

Bibliography

Allen, Roland. *Voluntary Clergy.* London: SPCK, 1923.
———. *The Case for Voluntary Clergy.* London: Eyre & Spottiswoode, 1930.
———. *Missionary Methods: St. Paul's or Ours?* Grand Rapids: Eerdmans, 1962.
———. *The Spontaneous Expansion of the Church: And the Causes That Hinder It.* Grand Rapids: Eerdmans, 1962.
Burnett, David. *Clash of Worlds.* Mill Hill, London: Monarch Books, 2002.
Coleman, Robert E. *The Master Plan of Evangelism.* Grand Rapids: Revell, 1993.
Corbett, Steve, and Brian Fikkert. *When Helping Hurts: How to Alleviate Poverty without Hurting the Poor and Yourself.* Chicago: Moody, 2009.
Daneel, M. L. *Quest for Belonging: Introduction to a Study of African Independent Churches.* Gweru, Zimbabwe: Mambo Press, 1987.
Dillion-Malone, Clive M. *The Korsten Basketmakers: A Study of the Masowe Apostles, an Indigenous African Religious Movement.* Manchester, England: Manchester University Press, 1978.
Guest, Robert. *The Shackled Continent: Africa's Past, Present, and Future.* London: Macmillan, 2004.
Harries, Jim. *Vulnerable Mission: Insights into Christian Mission to Africa from a Position of Vulnerability.* Pasadena, CA: William Carey, 2011.
Hatch, Nathan O. *The Democratization of American Christianity.* New Haven, CT: Yale University Press, 1989.
Hersey, Paul, and Kenneth H. Blanchard. *Management of Organizational Behavior: Utilizing Human Resources.* Fifth Edition. Englewood Cliffs, NJ: Prentice Hall, 1988.
Hiebert, Paul G. *Anthropological Insights for Missionaries.* Grand Rapids: Baker, 1985.
———. *Transforming Worldviews: An Anthropological Understanding of How People Change.* Grand Rapids: Baker Academic, 2008.
Hurtado, Larry W. *At the Origins of Christian Worship.* Grand Rapids: Eerdmans, 1999.
Jenkins, Philip. *The Next Christendom: The Coming of Global Christianity.* New York: Oxford University Press, 2002.
———. *The Lost History of Christianity: The Thousand-Year Golden Age of the Church in the Middle East, Africa, and Asia—and How It Died.* New York: HarperOne, 2008.
Ladd, George Eldon. "The Gospel of the Kingdom." In *Perspectives on the World Christian Movement: A Reader.* Third Edition. Edited by Ralph D. Winter and Steven C. Hawthorne, 64–77. Pasadena, CA: William Carey, 1999.
Martin, David. *Pentecostalism: The World Their Parish.* Malden, MA: Blackwell, 2002.
Moffett, Samuel Hugh. *A History of Christianity in Asia.* Vol. 2. *1500–1900.* Maryknoll, NY: Orbis, 2005.

Bibliography

Rauschenbusch, Walter. *Christianity and the Social Crisis.* Edited by Robert D. Cross. New York: Harper & Row, 1964.

Redpath, Alan. *Victorious Christian Service: Studies in the Book of Nehemiah.* Old Tappan, NJ: Fleming H. Revell, 1958.

Reese, Robert. "Johane Masowe." In *Dictionary of African Christian Biography.* www.dacb.org/stories/zimbabwe/johane_masowe.html, 2008.

———. *Roots and Remedies of the Dependency Syndrome in World Missions.* Pasadena, CA: William Carey, 2010.

Rowell, John. *To Give or Not To Give?: Rethinking Dependency, Restoring Generosity and Redefining Sustainability.* Tyrone, GA: Authentic, 2006.

Sanneh, Lamin. "The Horizontal and the Vertical in Mission: An African Perspective." *International Bulletin of Missionary Research* 7, no. 4 (October 1983): 165–71.

Schnabel, Eckhard J. *Paul the Missionary: Realities, Strategies and Methods.* Downers Grove, IL: IVP Academic, 2008.

Stott, John R. W. *Christian Mission in the Modern World.* Downers Grove, IL: InterVarsity, 1975.

Tempels, Placide. *Bantu Philosophy.* Paris: Presence Africaine, 1959.

Tennent, Timothy C. *Invitation to World Missions: A Trinitarian Missiology for the Twenty-First Century.* Grand Rapids: Kregel, 2010.

Van Rheenen, Gailyn. *Communicating Christ in Animistic Contexts.* Grand Rapids: Baker, 1991.

Walls, Andrew F. *The Cross-Cultural Process in Christian History.* Maryknoll, NY: Orbis, 2002.

www.ingramcontent.com/pod-product-compliance
Lightning Source LLC
Chambersburg PA
CBHW051102160426
43193CB00010B/1289